The Practitioner Inquiry Series

Marilyn Cochran-Smith and Susan L. Lytle, SERIES EDITORS

(continued)

Regarding Children's Words

TEACHER RESEARCH ON LANGUAGE AND LITERACY

BROOKLINE TEACHER RESEARCHER SEMINAR

Edited by Cynthia Ballenger
Foreword by Sarah Michaels

Teachers College, Columbia University
New York and London

Published by Teachers College Press, 1234 Amsterdam Avenue, New York, NY 10027

Library of Congress Cataloging-in-Publication Data

Regarding children's words : teacher research on language and literacy / Brookline Teacher Researcher Seminar ; edited by Cynthia Ballenger ; foreword by Sarah Michaels.
    p. cm. — (The practitioner inquiry series)
    Includes bibliographical references and index.
    ISBN 0-8077-4402-6 (cloth) — ISBN 0-8077-4401-8 (paper)
    1. Language arts (Elementary) 2. Action research in education. I. Ballenger, Cynthia. II. Brookline Teacher Researcher Seminar. III. Series.
    LB1576.R44 2004
    372.6—dc22   2003061152

ISBN 0-8077-4401-8 (paper)
ISBN 0-8077-4402-6 (cloth)

Contents

Foreword

In the decade-plus that the Brookline Teacher Researcher Seminar has been meeting, the term "teacher research" has steadily gained national and international prominence. But debates rage in the field of education about the nature and value of this kind of work. From the academy, to schools of education, to elementary schools and classrooms, we hear the following:

- What *is* teacher research?
- Is it one thing or is it many different things, depending on place, person, and purpose?
- Is it *really* research?
- Is it a form of qualitative, ethnographic research conducted by teachers, or is it an entirely new approach?
- What are the characteristics or the criteria or the elements of high-quality teacher research?
- How does one do it and what kind of knowledge does it produce?

As an academic (a sociolinguist by training), and as someone who has had the privilege of working with the members of the Brookline Teacher Researcher Seminar (BTRS) in its early years, I know that these questions do not have single or simple answers. In fact, many in the BTRS would say that these are not really the right questions to ask. Still, I think this book and the thinking of this remarkable group of teachers/ thinkers/writers have a great deal to say to all of us—academic researchers and researching teachers alike.

This book is the product of over ten years' work by the seminar members, who in their weekly meetings have developed, over time, a way of bringing their classrooms "to the table," so to speak. These educators have developed new ways of looking at, listening to, and learning from their students—and new ways of looking at, listening to, and learning from each other. And in both explaining and demonstrating the work, this book has the power to transform the way each of us thinks about teachers, students, classroom life, and the enterprise of research itself.

What makes this work so powerful? In my view, the mode of work developed in the BTRS—involving both processes and products—integrates and intermingles what Jerome Bruner, in his book *Actual Minds, Possible Worlds*, calls two distinct "modes of thought." Bruner describes these two modes, the logico-scientific (or paradigmatic) mode and the narrative mode, as follows:

> The paradigmatic or logico-scientific [mode] attempts to fulfill the ideal of a formal, mathematical system of description and explanation. It employs categorization or conceptualization and the operations by which categories are established, instantiated, idealized, and related one to the other to form a system . . . [using] devices by which general propositions are extracted from statements in the particular context. . . . The paradigmatic mode . . . seeks to transcend the particular by higher and higher reaching for abstraction. . . .
>
> The . . . narrative mode leads instead to good stories, gripping drama, believable (though not necessarily "true") historical accounts. It deals in human or human-like intention and action and the vicissitudes and consequences that mark their course. It strives to put its timeless miracles into the particulars of experience, and to locate the experience of time and place. (pp. 12–13)

Bruner suggests that these two modes are "different natural kinds, . . . distinctive ways of ordering experience, or constructing reality." He suggests that "efforts to reduce one mode to the other or to ignore one at the expense of the other inevitably fail to capture the rich diversity of thought" (p. 11).

What is uniquely powerful about the work of the BTRS is that they have found a way to constructively blend these two modes of thought, holding in binocular vision—at one and the same time—concrete particulars of classroom life and abstract generalizations about children and about teaching and learning. A similar phenomenon of blending is pointed to in Gallas' chapter where she quotes Medawar in his description of the actions of scientists:

> Scientific reasoning is . . . at all levels an interaction between two episodes of thought—a dialogue between two voices, the one imaginative and the other critical; a dialogue . . . between the possible and the actual, between proposal and disposal, between what might be true and what is in fact the case. (1982, p. 46)

Most educational researchers have found it impossible to integrate these two modes, or at least to do so in compelling, credible, and rigorous ways. The teacher researchers from the BTRS have found both practices and products that allow for this compelling and instructive (and in the end, transformative) integration.

How do they do it? Much of the book is an answer to this question, but I want to point to one aspect of their work: their way of working together as colleagues.

From early on in the work of the BTRS—perhaps because many of the founding members were interested in understanding students' understanding through their talk—the group began to bring tape-recorders into their classrooms, and then the tapes and transcripts from these recordings into the seminar. It became a primary way of "bringing their classrooms to the table" for one another.

One important window, thus, was through the lens of "literacies as talk." They emphasized the kind of talk and text, the ways with words, that were engendered in their classrooms, and in particular, their role as orchestrators of that talk. They developed practices for "stopping time" and slowing down their interpretive processes so that they could look at what they said and what expectations for talk (often implicit and subtle) they held, as well as at the "ways with words" their students brought to the table. In addressing particular episodes of talk, they tend to focus particular attention on those students whom they find it hard to connect with, hard to co-construct meaning with. It often turns out that these are the same students who are not successful participants (at the outset) of the classroom conversation.

From the start, this kind of teacher research has focused on the ways that the teachers missed or misjudged their students' understandings, rather than the things they got right. The work seemed to create a space for talking honestly about puzzles, frustrations, mistakes. And the work with the "texts" of talk led the teachers back into their classroom, with more questions, and heightened interest in making space for these students to demonstrate their ways of making meaning. This in turn generated new "texts" and, often, new discourse spaces in the classroom, new opportunities to see students in action, and new opportunities for both teacher and student learning. The practice of studying transcripts as data has served as a catalyst for deriving new understandings of the strengths of these students, harnessing and refining analytic tools for satisfactorily treating the data, as well as developing new ways of seeing and understanding the complex process of the co-construction of meaning between teachers and students in a classroom, and with colleagues outside of the classroom.

There are two key aspects of this practice that bear more discussion: 1) the emphasis on sharing "raw data" (in the form of audio or video recordings, or students' texts) as opposed to anecdotes about what happened on a particular occasion or as a regular occurence; and 2) the emphasis on collegial review of one's own data.

The benefits are multiple and multi-faceted:

- People bring to the table what I think of as "raw data"—not already interpreted accounts or anecdotes of what works or what doesn't, but the rich, unedited, messy talk of real classrooms, with all the false starts, interruptions, and missed opportunities. They bring transcripts full of hard-to-interpret or even incoherent remarks, produced on the fly. But when the transcripts are revisited, it usually turns out students are making powerful sense. Rehearing what was said (via the laborious process of transcribing a tape) and re-seeing talk in a transcript becomes a way to give reason to your students. It's a way to give students more time and space to be heard, and it allows the teacher to step back and assess his or her own role and responsibility in creating the discourse space. In practice, it has often led to increased trust and connection between teacher and students, ultimately allowing them to build new meaning together.

- Because these teacher researchers come together as colleagues to do this work, it allows multiple perspectives to be brought to bear on the data—though the data are still one's own. The teacher has far more insider knowledge of the situation, the students, and hence the right to knowledge claims about what's happening and what it means. The collaborative process, in my experience, turns out to be far more transformative than reflection in isolation. The group works to push each other further—making the familiar strange, rethinking what's possible, and coming to value their students as having powerful minds and cogent arguments, although perhaps not always fully explicated or expressed in the ways teachers were expecting.

The process of bringing transcripts to the table with colleagues creates a space that typically doesn't exist in the context of teacher lounges, faculty meetings, or even professional development seminars on teaching. It often allows one to "see" one's own world in concert with the experiences, vantage point, interests, and tools of others, while remaining in command of the data and the ultimate interpretations that result. It allows the teacher researcher to take from the collective resources of the community all that seems helpful and reasonable.

By the nature of the "game" of bringing one's classroom to the table with colleagues, the others looking at the data are positioned as allies, not outside critics or, as is typical in scholarly work, as blind reviewers. They too will bring their data to the table; this builds a reciprocity that induces trust and a willingness to expose problems, rather than merely touting one's own successes. In my experience with the BTRS and with other groups of teachers inspired by this work, this kind of discourse space can build bridges across grade levels, disciplines, even institutional boundaries, and creates an environment where people explore problematic aspects of practice that they would not ordinarily expose publicly. I have seen elementary school teachers work as valued co-researchers with senior academics, and just as remarkable, high school teachers working side-by-side with elementary special ed teachers. In several places, this kind of work has been sustained (with no outside funding) over many years simply because it turns out to be so intellectually rewarding and productive. The work inspired by the BTRS has even spread, in some cases, to university contexts. One Clark University English professor claims it pushed him to radically rethink his own teaching—for the first time in his entire career. A math professor (who began this work as a content advisor to school teachers) began videotaping his own classes and claims he now hears things in students' words he never heard before. This work seems to create a space where divergent worlds come together, intermingle, and create the possibility for new understandings—new understandings of the data but also of one another and of one's students.

How do these teacher researchers analyze "classroom practice"? What do they look for? Typically, the work proceeds with primacy given to transcripts of talk and examples of students' writing (a kind of self-collecting data). Of course transcripts/texts don't in and of themselves "speak" to you. "Seeing" what's in the transcript requires a meta-language and set of analytic tools, tools which enable you to see patterns, significance. And of course, a transcript inevitably leaves out a lot of information (non-verbal, intonational information, but also information with respect to students' class, classroom status, etc.). And bringing a piece of student work to the table strips it of all of the social interactions that surrounded and shaped the text—the "text" of the assignment, class discussion, collaborative work, etc. (Michaels, 1987). The seemingly precise tools for analyzing talk and text, counting and coding, can just as easily blind you to some of the patterns. Looking at words per turn, for example, can be very misleading as an indicator of quality of talk. There is no simple set of tools or approaches for determining the constructs one emphasizes, the decisions one makes as to what counts as a key situation, how representative it is of others like it, how many instances of it you need to collect, and what units of analysis are appropriate. These have been long standing, vexing problems—for the BTRS teachers as well as experienced classroom discourse analysts or experienced scholars of literary texts (see Gee et al., 1992). These challenges have often spurred the group to seek outside expertise—soliciting the assistance of academic colleagues in some cases, or reading articles by linguists, sociologists, or literary critics. The result, however, of looking at transcripts in disciplined ways allows, over time, for rich and compelling analyses of "data"—informed by many different perspectives and analytic tools—as embedded in the particular stories of real teacher and real students over time.

And as the BTRS teachers show us in their chapters, the process is iterative. Puzzling over a transcript collectively, or in Phillips' words, "taking a turn," suggests questions and even theoretical frameworks for understanding the "text." This sends one back into the classroom with new questions and interests, generating new interactions and pedagogical practices, new transcripts, new analyses, and support for (or in some cases, undermining) the value of one's theoretical or analytic framework. It is this recursive practice or "form of life" that, in my view, creates a dialogue between "the possible and the actual . . . between what might be true and what is in fact the case" (Medawar, 1982, p. 46). And it is what makes the work so compelling as a story, and so informative and transformative as empirical research.

In short, the practices and products of the BTRS show us both "the actual" (the problematic and messy) while giving us ways to imagine (and act to bring about) "the possible"—a way of making school a productive, transformative place for both children and adults.

—Sarah Michaels

Acknowledgments

An earlier version of Chapter 3 first appeared as "Now the Robbers Is Nice" in *Teaching Other People's Children: Literacy and Learning in a Bilingual Classroom* (pp. 69–81) by Cynthia Ballenger, published by Teachers College Press. Copyright © 1999 by Teachers College, Columbia University. Reprinted by permission.

An earlier version of Chapter 5 first appeared as "In Search of an Honest Response" by Jim Swaim in *Language Arts*, vol. 75, no. 2, pp. 118–125. Copyright © 1999 by the National Council of Teachers of English. Reprinted by permission.

An earlier version of Chapter 8 first appeared as "Look, Karen, I'm Running Like Jello: Imagination as a Question, a Topic, a Tool for Literacy Research and Learning" by Karen Gallas in *Research in the Teaching of English*, vol. 35, no. 4. Copyright © 2001 by the National Council of Teachers of English. Reprinted by permission.

We would also like to acknowledge funding from the Mellon Foundation to the Literacies Institute, which assisted us in our work, and funding from the Spencer Foundation, which assisted us in writing this book.

Regarding Children's Words

TEACHER RESEARCH
ON
LANGUAGE AND LITERACY

Developing a Community of Inquiry: The Values and Practices of the Brookline Teacher Researcher Seminar

ANN PHILLIPS AND KAREN GALLAS

The Three Robbers by Tomi Ungerer (1991) was the book that the children loved above all others. From the first day we read it, they talked about it, pored over the pictures pretending to read, and carried it around with them during the school day. I could see clearly that it was important to them. And yet it was a long time before we ever managed to finish it. As I read, they would constantly interrupt. The discussion would go far afield and although I tried to bring us back to the book, I rarely succeeded. The children were too excited, too interested in what they were talking about.

—Cynthia Ballenger, Chapter 3, this volume

We begin our introduction to this book with an excerpt from Cynthia Ballenger's study of storybook reading because her words exemplify the unique aspects of the most important body of work in this book, research by teachers. First, the research that led to Cindy's written commentary was rooted in classroom practice at a moment when this experienced teacher's best practices simply did not work. And it was rooted in a series of moments of puzzlement, and in delight and wonder at the words and worlds of children. Further, Cindy gained these insights, not in a moment, but over a sustained period of time; she recorded these moments in field notes and transcriptions of tape-recorded classroom interactions, capturing words and actions that otherwise might have escaped her in the never-ending press of time in the classroom. Most notably perhaps, the impetus for Cindy's work was a deep and abiding interest in classroom talk, and in the barriers to understanding children that differences in language and culture often impose. Finally, Cindy's classroom practice did not take place in isolation; she brought her questions, her stories, her data, and her vulnerability to the weekly meetings of the Brookline Teacher Researcher Seminar (BTRS), whose members, teachers and sociolinguists, shared Cindy's concern for equity, her delight with children, and her respect for teaching as a complex, essential, and uncertain profession.

The heart of this book is research by teachers, final accounts developed from observations like Cindy Ballenger's above. The chapters presenting those accounts represent various moments on one journey that included at times different metaphors, engagement with different literature, and different problems. Those chapters are, however, preceded by two that paint a portrait of the workings of the BTRS as a group. In this introductory chapter, we hope to reveal to the reader the members' understanding, as it developed over time, of the larger enterprise they were engaged in, as teachers and as researchers: the effort to make *talk* visible in the classroom.

The methodology that we describe was not born of pure intellectual inquiry. Its seeds were planted in actual meetings between teachers and academic researchers: Sarah Michaels, Mary Catherine O'Connor, and James Gee. These meetings actually involve a complex web of connections, interactions, and ideas. To describe this complex web fully would require a book of its own. What follows is an example of the kind of encounter in which the BTRS developed its approach to teacher research.

OUR INQUIRY INTO CHILDREN'S LANGUAGE

Early History of the BTRS

In 1984, Steve Griffin joined the staff of an elementary school in Brookline, Massachusetts as a speech and language therapist. To his surprise, when he began the school year he found that the children referred to him for therapy in this predominantly middle- and upper-middle-class professional community included most of the African-American students who attended the school. Moreover, by November the teachers who had referred those students to Steve began telling him that many of the same students were writing extraordinary poems as part of their work with a poet who was artist-in-residence. So Steve found himself with a troubling contradiction: Why were students who were so skillful in their use of poetic language being referred for language therapy? What would become the Brookline Teacher Research Seminar began with a teacher's question.

Steve began to look for help in thinking about this contradiction. He eventually decided to enroll in the linguistics program at Boston University where he knew that academics like Jim Gee were deeply interested in language, culture, and equity. Jim's own work, which addresses the capacity of every human being to make sense (Gee, 1989a, b, c), spoke powerfully to Steve's concerns. Likewise, Steve's work and his knowledge of schools spoke powerfully to Jim. Although Jim is a linguist, not a teacher, he believed that it was urgent that schools address the contradictions that Steve had noticed. Jim had a deep interest in and respect for Steve's question.

Steve and Jim and Sarah Michaels had the opportunity to develop a practical framework for exploring these mutual interests and concerns when the Mellon Foundation accepted Jim's and Sarah's proposal for the funding of the Literacies Institute. Sarah, an ethnographer and sociolinguist, shared Jim's and Steve's concern for equity. Sarah and Jim shared a perspective on language that shed light on Steve's observations, but neither he nor they knew how this theoretical perspective would influence the practice of teachers who shared Steve's concerns.

As a result, Steve urged Sarah, as chair of the Literacies Institute, to move quickly to meet with practicing teachers on a regular basis. Thus the seed for the BTRS was sown, and in 1988 Sarah Michaels and Steve Griffin convened a pilot group for what eventually became the community of teachers and researchers that has met weekly since the spring of 1989. Steve, in the course of this work, became a classroom teacher rather than a speech and language therapist.

In the spring of 1989, as everyone present began to grope for ways in which the ideas of sociolinguists might serve the needs of the classroom, Sarah told another story, similar in some ways to Steve's, and embodied in a paper entitled "Hearing the Connections in Children's Oral and written Discourse" (Michaels, 1985). In this paper Sarah examined two literacy activities: sharing time and a writing conference. She contrasted two African-American children's elaborate narrative intentions with their teachers' goals for more linear, topic-centered stories. Using her knowledge as a sociolinguist, she showed how the intentions of the African-American students were more complex than the teachers realized or were expecting, thus leading to missed opportunities for both teachers to help their respective students develop their ideas. In her conclusion, Sarah called for approaches that place teachers in the role of "respectful listeners" who do not require children to sacrifice complex ideas for the sake of "literate-like language" (p. 53).

This paper struck a familiar chord for many of us who recognized that the dynamic being described existed in our own classrooms. In our classrooms and through readings we began to pay careful attention to the language barriers that hid children's ideas. Several published papers on classroom discourse were read and discussed (Delpit, 1986, 1988; Gee, 1989a, 1989b, 1989c; Heath, 1982, 1983; Michaels, 1982, 1985; Paley, 1986), and we began to pose practical questions. Sarah had tape-recorded the classroom activities in her research as an observer, not as a teacher. She was not subject to the pace and flow of classroom life. How could we create the time and space to uncover what was visible to Sarah only after painstaking research in which she examined the transcription of a tape-recorded event time and time again in order to understand it? Moreover, how could we capture those interactions? How and when would we find the opportunity to even turn on a tape-recorder? Sarah asked Steve Griffin to try to tape-record an interaction with a child in his classroom.

"Seeing" Complex Thought

Sarah transcribed the tape-recording from Steve's classroom and brought it to the group for consideration. Steve was working on a math story problem with his second-grade student, Megan, who proposed the number sentence, $2 - 4 = 20$. Had Steve been "teaching", that is, covering the curriculum in a timely manner, rather than researching her ideas, he might have ended the interaction by helping Megan see the problem with such a number sentence. However, because the purpose of Steve's work was to research rather than to teach, he spoke less in this interaction than he might normally have, and he listened more. Megan's later explanations, combined with the group's work to understand what she meant, revealed a significant understanding of the story problem, which the number sentence did not suggest by itself. Her mathematical thinking would not have been visible in normal classroom interaction. This experience suggested how normal teaching practice can stand in the way of seeing the complexity of children's thought, and it led us to a heightened awareness of the teacher's role in uncovering or obscuring it.

The Power of the Observer

As those early meetings progressed, our interests shifted toward our own classrooms, and with technical advice about managing the tape recorder in the classroom, we each began to record interactions in our respective settings. As we turned the spotlight on ourselves, we discovered the power of observation to change the nature of our interactions with children. A discussion in our fourth session that spring highlighted both the teacher's power to control an interaction and the power of observation to help the teacher "see" that interaction. In that meeting Betsy Kellogg (1990) reported on a small piece of research from her classroom.

> At one point the woman who works in my classroom took notes while I was sitting with kids doing a math problem. It was great in terms of what we talked about last time in terms of waiting, and, as a teacher, after looking back through the transcripts I learned how much I "overlead" them. How much I know what I am looking for so I immediately, even when the beginning letter starts correctly, I jump on them and say, "Ah, you were going to say 40, weren't you?" even when they were going to say something completely different. That was an awakening!

In the previous session we had spoken about how difficult it was to learn what children were thinking. In this session Betsy illuminated the process through which she and other teachers limited their own access to a child's knowledge and understanding by "overleading," anticipating a child's words and limiting the child's opportunity to speak. This example was the first of many in which we commented on our control of talk in the classroom.

Betsy's comment about the effect that her partner's note taking had on her interaction also led to a discussion of how an observer affects teaching. Just as examining the transcript of another teacher had frozen the action, an observer—in the form of an individual, an audiotape, or a videotape—had the power to bring to our minds a new way of interacting with children. As time passed, we learned that the content of our meetings, individual members' stories, and the transcripts we deciphered with delight, came back with us into the classroom and played the role of observer as well.

Entering a Research Discipline

In the fall of 1989, we were introduced to the research tools of sociolinguistics and ethnography by Ann Phillips, with the support of Sarah Michaels and Cathy O'Connor. When it came time to study discourse analysis, Sarah and Cathy lead the session. As the meeting progressed, Sarah and Cathy broke their longstanding resolution not to dominate discussions in the seminar, and they became intensely engaged in discussing and questioning the meaning of a transcript of science talk from Karen Gallas' classroom. Sarah and Cathy's practice of discourse analysis was complex. It could not be reduced to a protocol. The two features of their work that most affected us as teachers were: the careful way in which they attended to each word a child uttered, and the joy they took from examining a child's words. Along with what we learned about these habits of mind and the practices of discourse analysis, it was this delight at the work and words of children that fueled our early explorations.

Our driving questions about classroom discourse emerged at that time: How do schools conceive of competence and skill in language use? What does this view leave out? What do children, especially minority and culturally diverse children, bring to the classroom that this conceptualization overlooks? What do children who are placed in special education classrooms bring to the classroom that this conceptualization overlooks? What is the value of the diversity of children's language styles for thought, for imagination, for the construction of classroom communities?

Values and Practices

We discovered through a recursive process of ethnography and reflections the existence of unique discourse or talk processes. As we identified the practices and their larger meaning in the community, we gave them names. In this section we introduce those terms to assist the reader in understanding the underlying values and practices that shaped each of the investigations presented in this book.

Silence. Silence may be the most prominent feature of the seminar; almost all visitors and all new members were struck and bewildered by this practice. It originated in Ann Phillips's own teaching practice, and under her leadership that year it became an embedded discourse practice in our community. Ann consciously adopted the practice of waiting for seminar members to speak, rather than filling in silences between remarks with her own commentary or questions. As we worked together, we observed that this practice created time and space for each of us to form new and unexpected ideas. Subsequently, a number of us decided that a central investigative tool to use in our research would be the creation of a similar, open discourse space in the classroom, one that provided expanded time for students to talk and for their peers to respond and for many of them to reveal themselves more fully. Many of the chapters in this book describe the creation of those kinds of spaces and the ways in which they propelled our investigations forward and changed our practice as teachers. We want to emphasize that this practice of using silence to create open discourse spaces remained in our minds as a point to explore.

Stopping Time. In the seminar, as silence became a kind of research protocol, it also "stopped time" (Phillips, 1991) by creating space where our knowledge and our questions about teaching could surface. We were able to snatch further moments from the rapid progression of events in the classroom when we discovered that the taping itself, and then the collaborative and respectful consideration of the transcript with colleagues, "froze the action." Our collaborative investigations spanned a great deal of time and included various activities, such as multiple presentations of data through memos, group reflections on readings, and group readings of each seminar member's account of his or her investigation prior to the presentation of a paper. The opportunity to revisit our work not only once, but as often as was necessary, was one way that we virtually stopped time.

Exploratory Talk. The discourse practices associated with our community again developed in association with our research practices. One practice that first developed in seminar meetings and then became a focus of our classroom research was exploratory talk (Barnes, 1976). The intention of this kind of talk is to develop knowledge, not to display what the speaker already knows and understands. Exploratory talk is thinking out-loud, so to speak, and the pace of exploratory talk is unusually slow because the speaker is exploring ideas. Thus, exploratory talk both requires silence and creates it. If an observer is not used to such talk or does not understand its purposes, he or she may believe that the speaker is unsure of him- or herself. Exploratory talk requires the courage to accept and display the limitations of one's knowledge. It creates not only an opportunity to "stop time" temporally, but also an opportunity to "stop time" mentally, so that new ways of thinking, unencumbered by ideology or previous assumptions, can develop.

The Puzzling Event. The "puzzling event" is the name we have given to the moment when we realize that something going on in our classroom is amazing, doesn't make sense, or wasn't predicted from

our past experience. Cindy Beseler records in her field notes an example
of just such an experience.

> As we walked down the street to [the hospital] the kids made a
> "Cindy sandwich" on either side of me. They do not do that at
> school. Rebecca leaned on my shoulder and teased me by
> pretending to push me into lampposts. They would not do that
> to a teacher at school. The guys followed suit and I reacted
> differently to a male hanging on my shoulder. . . . I felt very
> unprofessional. I know I'm respectfully honoring a very impor-
> tant kind of learning that develops only in private spaces. I just
> wonder if I'm not disrupting their learning in the public space.

Cindy describes here a tension she feels about her teaching. Her developmentally delayed students are playing with language and with their
social roles. And yet she knows they also need help learning how to
use the language required in formal and public situations. In subsequent meetings, with encouragement from seminar members, the anec-
dote expanded and the questions that surrounded her observation
surfaced. Eventually she was led to collect data and systematically study
the various functions for language that her students found in their lives
and the role of play in learning these functions. From such puzzling
events, often moments of tension or frustration initially, most of the
research in this book derives.

Valuing Confusion. Often in schools, a teacher's statement of confusion is seen as evidence of lack of expertise and is met with proffered
solutions and/or practical suggestions for new teaching techniques to
try. In the seminar, however, an acknowledgment of confusion was
met with encouragement to remain open to uncertainty, to identify
the questions behind the confusion, and to return to the classroom
and seek more data in relation to those questions. We see this in Cindy
Ballenger's words that begin this book.

When we begin to research a classroom interaction, often our assumptions about what has taken place are turned upside down. Just as
an ethnographer immersed in a new culture experiences confusion
before illuminating stories or patterns begin to emerge, so, too, the
practice of classroom ethnography requires an openness to seeing new
patterns and relationships in the daily events of our classrooms.

Big Ideas. Similarly, since our inception we have come in contact
with theoretical work that stimulated our interest, both as points of

departure for research questions and/or as frameworks from which to expand our understanding of what we were seeing in our data. New perspectives most commonly were brought into the group by individual members who would, in their outside reading, come upon papers that were provocative and bring them to the seminar for discussion. In this way we came in contact with work on stories and sense making (Dyson, 1989, 1993; Gee, 1989a, 1989b; Heath, 1982, 1983; Paley, 1986; Wells, 1986); on classroom discourse (Barnes, 1976; Cazden, 1988; Delpit, 1986, 1988); and on the social construction of language in and across cultures (Bakhtin, 1981; Gee, 1990; Morson & Emerson, 1990). These influences will be evident in the chapters that follow.

A Word for Our Readers About Teacher Research

Although the term *teacher research* may suggest that inquiry into practice by teachers is similar to inquiry into practice by academic researchers, it is not. As Bakhtin (1984), Heath (1982), and others have pointed out, ways of using language are shaped by the needs of the particular community in which they occur. As in other research communities, one of the purposes of our teacher research group is to uncover important knowledge about language in order to improve the lives of the children we teach, but our histories as teachers, the conditions in which we worked, and the community that shapes that work are different from those of academic researchers. Thus, in the seminar, we have found a terminology emerging directly from our spiraling discussions about language, literacy, and the lives of the children we taught as they were represented in our data. For example, seminar members speak about the "shadow curriculum" (Ballenger, 1999), and about "subtextual dynamics" (Gallas, 1998), undercurrents of social, emotional, and intellectual life, that subtly affect learning and teaching. We refer to "I Need People" stories as an exemplar of how talk requires community, and we search for "the honest response" (Swaim, 1998) as a measure of the engagement of that community. These are open, metaphoric terms reflecting the messiness of social relations, the unpredictability of classroom events, the charged mental and physical energy that runs below the surface of classroom life, and they embody our deeply held belief that children bring uncommon understanding and insight to their learning.

Readers of this book will not find commonly used terms from more traditional educational research in the chapters that follow. We will not speak about generalizable findings, replicability, models, paradigms, and objectivity. This does not mean that our work is atheoretical or anti-intellectual, or that it cannot be applied to many different kinds of classrooms in diverse settings. But it does mean that we believe the language of educational research must come to reflect an "intermingling of voices" (Phillips, 1993), an inclusive discourse that both teachers and researchers will recognize as emanating from the heart of their work. We believe that heart is found in the local, in the conversational, in the action and prosaics of classrooms. It is our hope that the way in which we present our theoretical positions and the descriptions that accompany them will resonate with all of our readers, laying the groundwork for more complete understandings of how teachers and students in different settings build inclusive discourse communities.

OVERVIEW OF THE BOOK

Chapter 1, "Turns in a Conversation," is by Ann Phillips, our ethnographer. The heart of the chapter is an examination of a teacher's research project, what came to be called a *turn*. As ethnographer, Ann often contemplated the meaning of the group's practices and through her writing presented these to the group to see if they rang true. The term *turn* was picked up and developed by the community over time.

Then follow the classroom narratives, beginning with Steve Griffin's story, because the group began with him. Chapter 2, "I Need People," exemplifies our early and powerful realization that a research perspective could help us to develop a broader and more complicated view of language use and children's strengths and goals in this regard. Steve's story is an account of a new and powerful genre of storytelling that developed as he studied sharing time in his first-grade classroom.

The remaining chapters take this perspective into various domains, bilingual classrooms, special education settings, writing workshop, sharing time. In each chapter the teacher asks, What sense are the children making of what we are asking them to do? The teacher strives to ask this question in an open manner, no matter what label her students carry. In each case, the children are doing something both serious and important, and something from which we learn.

In "Reading Storybooks with Young Children" (Chapter 3) Cindy Ballenger takes this concern into her work as a teacher of Haitian preschoolers. A central part of her practice was to read storybooks. And yet this time-honored early childhood practice did not look the same as it had in other classroom where she had taught. The children in this group cheerfully defied her expectations and caused her to develop a more complicated understanding of children's, and adults', response to stories.

In Chapter 4, "Students Talking and Writing Their Way into 'Functional' Worlds," Cindy Beseler explores the language her delayed high schoolers use when she is not taking a conventional teacher's role. She documents the ways in which her students speak and write in relation to different contexts, and the powerful and unexpected competencies they have when the setting is under their control.

In Chapter 5, "In Search of an Honest Response," Jim Swaim explores the structure of the writing process in his third-grade classroom. He delves into moments when he feels he has failed to provide an environment where his students can learn to connect deeply with literature, and narrates how he was able to change his practice, with the help of his students.

Chapter 6, "What's Real About Imagination?" by Roxanne Pappenheimer chronicles another dialogic journey, moving back and forth between her assumptions about the imaginations of her developmentally delayed students and what the students were able to show her about their need for literature. Her piece poses questions to all of us about how we imagine other lives and what happens when reality intercedes.

Susan Black-Donellan is a special educator who was, as she explains in Chapter 7, "Mainstreaming," very much in favor of mainstreaming and certain that it was good for her students. Why was it then that they seemed to dislike it so much? Interviewing them, and reflecting on what they told her, gave her a new and more complicated perspective on this practice.

Karen Gallas reports in Chapter 8, "Look, Karen, I'm Running Like Jello," on the role of the imagination in learning. She analyzes children's activity in public spheres, such as music and storytelling performances, as well as their more private dramas and proposes new ways to see the crucial role that imagination plays in children's learning and identity as thinkers.

CHAPTER 1

Turns in a Conversation: An Exemplar of a Project in the BTRS

ANN PHILLIPS

CONVERSATION AS A CONCEPTUAL FRAMEWORK

It was my colleague Steve Griffin, a second-grade teacher and founding member of the BTRS, who coined the term *orchestrating the voices*. This phrase brings into relief the responsibility of a leader to ensure that everyone be heard. He used this term when describing my role as BTRS chair. I was leading a conversation among adults—teachers and academic researchers—who shared the common goal of ensuring that all children genuinely be heard and understood in the classroom. I was assigned the task of creating a "public space" in which we could attend to one another and talk about our practice with "interest, regard, and care" (Greene, 1988, p. 19).

As I tried to do this, I found myself more and more aware of the human desire not only to speak, but also to speak in the rhythms of one's own voice, from one's own concerns, and from the knowledge of a lifetime of work. I became more fully aware of the human desire to say what one knows and cares about, in the way that one is used to speaking. This is what Maxine Greene calls "a space of possibility" (1988, p. 19), and what Israel Scheffler calls "voice" (1984, pp. 154). It was at this point—as I was searching for how to attend to what teachers wanted to say about teaching when they were given the chance to speak, that the term *voice* became important to me.

Joe McDonald brought my attention to the teacher's voice, beginning with Israel Scheffler's introduction of the term in his contribution to the *Harvard Educational Review*'s symposium on the educational reports of 1983 (Scheffler, 1984). McDonald was a high school teacher and the documentalist of the Secondary Study Group (SSG), a group of teachers who met for many years to discuss their practice together. McDonald (1986) amplified Scheffler's use of the term with his own definition and with his rich account of teachers' voices in his article on the SSG, "Raising the Teacher's Voice and the Ironic Role of Theory." Scheffler (1984), noting the absence of teachers in the preparation of the educational reports mentioned above, insisted that teachers participate in preparing social documents about their work. He noted that this absence created a substantial weakness in these reports because they omitted the central players in the field of education. He described the unique view of teachers and pointed out that they should be viewed as "subjects—active beings whose field of endeavor is structured by their own symbolic systems, their conceptions of world, self, and community, their memories of past, perceptions of the present, and hopes for the future." He called this "hearing them in their own voice" (pp. 154–155). McDonald (1986) also used the term *voice* "in the sense of a sound full of meaning for those who will only listen," adding, "But at the same time I use it in a subtly different way, in a way that highlights the uttering of the voice, the very power to utter, rather than the content and meaning of the utterance" (p. 7).

Thus, Scheffler signaled the unique position that teachers occupy by virtue of their practice, their experience, and their labor in the world. McDonald added the concrete sense of voice, the physical quality of "uttering" the sound. In his account of the discussions held among the teachers of the Secondary Study Group, he situated the teachers talking together against the background of their long silence about teaching, and he described the evolution of their group from a stage when they were "just talking" to a stage when they talked "to know what they knew." His study is rich with transcripts and illuminates an important sequence of events. First, teachers spoke together and then, through the power of their collective voices, spoke to policy makers and theorists. Finally, they reached a point where they decided to claim and mine what they knew as teachers. McDonald's study points to the powerful role of actual talk in gaining "voice," in Scheffler's sense.

McDonald's attention to the power of speech, and the necessity to speak, resonated with my experience as a witness to teachers' desire to be fully heard and to speak in their own voices. I suspect that even people who have the power to speak freely in many contexts have experienced the pain of not knowing when or how to speak, or of not being heard. I choose to use the concept of a *conversation* as an organizing idea for this account of the practices that developed in the BTRS. I use this term because I have observed that in certain situations it is the form of speech to which we turn when we wish to affirm and invite others to speak fully.

When we choose the term *to converse*, I believe that we are evoking one of its very early meanings, that is, "to abide or dwell with others" (Oxford English Dictionary), evoking a physical presence, or willingness to attend to another that might allow us to hear what the other intends to say. I say this not to imply that conversation is an ideal form, or that all attempts at conversation are satisfactory to the participants, but rather to evoke the intention to listen, to attend, and to care that accompanies what is called a "good conversation."

Conversation is social. People have conversations in order to connect to one another and to comment in some way on the larger social world outside their conversation. In a conversation, people seek to be heard, to have what they say taken up and affirmed by at least one other participant. The participants seek to speak in their own voices, that is, from the knowledge of their lived lives. In the case of teachers, they speak from the knowledge of their work. I do not suggest that one often is fully heard, or even that one has a single "voice," because we all have multiple experiences of the world, and time is limited. We all know that each conversation has its own implicit rules for determining who may speak and what they may speak about, but because conversation seeks to be inclusive, both the rules and the process of taking turns, of determining who speaks and what the topic of the conversation is, may shift.

In a casual conversation on the street, these shifts are often subtle and implicit; the participants decide on the shifts mutually. In more formal conversation, the turns and the topics may be orchestrated, with the goal of creating opportunities for all the participants to feel included, to know that they have a right to speak and something to speak about. An example of this situation is a dinner party at which not everyone knows one another. If the conversation is not orchestrated so that connections are revealed and topics of mutual interest are put on the table, it is possible that a few of the guests will speak to one another about an experience of mutual interest, while the others merely listen. However, if someone deliberately creates an opportunity for another to speak (by asking a question, for example) or takes a turn to point out mutual connections, each person may find a point of entry into the conversation. Such orchestration of a conversation may seem transparent, but it reflects a desire to see that all participants are affirmed in some way.

THE BROOKLINE TEACHER RESEARCHER SEMINAR

I turn now to a description of conversation in the Brookline Teacher Researcher Seminar. The data for this description were derived from my 7 years of firsthand experience as member, occasional leader, and documentalist of the group. This analysis is drawn from interviews, transcripts, and published and unpublished written work (Ballenger, 1999; Gallas, 1991, 1994, 1995; Griffin, 1990a, 1990b; Phillips, 1990, 1991, 1993, 1994; Phillips et al., 1993).

Setting

The first six meetings of the group were held at the Education Development Center (EDC), a large office building that housed the Literacies Institute. Teachers traveled there from their school systems in Brookline and Cambridge. However, when the group began to meet the next year, it found its characteristic setting: a classroom in a public school. Since that time, the group has met in classrooms, except when a lack of heating, or a teachers' labor dispute, has made school buildings off limits. At these times, the group meets in members' homes. Food is always served, a "snack" that is brought in turn by each group member. Snack time is an invariable and essential part of the meeting.

Participants

The seminar consists of a group of teachers and researchers who meet weekly. As described in the introduction to this volume, in the beginning the group included Michaels, eight teachers, and myself. All of the teachers except me, were working full time. I had begun full-time graduate study the previous semester after 20 years of classroom teaching. Over the next 6 years, the composition of the group changed as members left or joined, but the mix of teachers and researchers has continued to the present.

In addition to these participants, the BTRS places great value on its virtual participants. Cindy Ballenger, the second teacher leader of the BTRS, began the first meeting of the year by introducing "those of us who aren't present" to new members. Cindy was not referring to members who were absent that day. Rather, she meant children, who might never have been physically present, but whose voices members had heard over time on audio recordings. Most were students of teachers in the group, and one was a child whom Sarah Michaels had brought to the seminar through her paper.

After Cindy introduced the children, she introduced previous members, theorists, and writers, some of whom the group had met, Jim Gee, for example, but others known only through their writing, including

Courtney Cazden, Shirley Brice Heath, Douglas Barnes, Lisa Delpit, Vivian Paley, Sylvia Ashton-Warner, and others.

Cindy's introductions had two purposes. First, she wanted to point out a phenomenon that the group had noticed: that the children and the others had become a constant source of not only delight but reflection. A child, the work of members, and the words of theorists continued to live in the considerations of individual and group members. Second, Cindy, as representative of the group, expressed the BTRS's desire to be inclusive. She wanted new members to "know" these participants. Several teachers had joined the BTRS that year and, as always, the group was conscious that older members might exclude these new members through the references made to past experiences and to virtual participants.

Finally, the group had another source of virtual, and occasionally local, participants. These came from the group's funding. Site visits from board members were one source of participants, as was a constant awareness of the wishes, needs, and views of the funders.

Methods

The thread of interest and investigation that was sustained over the years in this group was focused on finding a way to step outside the rush of events of the classroom to understand better what children have to say. The BTRS consciously sought a *methodology* for looking at language in the classroom. They chose to learn about the techniques of ethnography and sociolinguistics in order to develop such a methodology. These methods and the epistemological framework that they represented were never intended to suffice or remain the same. Rather, they served as a point of entry into a conversation with academic researchers who had used these methods, and they served as a point of departure for practitioners to look at children's complex intentions and their forms of expression and ultimately to "theorize" about what they learned.

The journey opened a new landscape in which the group came to examine not only children's intentions, but also teachers' intentions and intuitions. Over time the focus shifted from an individual child's intentions and interaction with the teacher, to the classroom as a community in which children's intentions and ways of talking (discourse) were accepted or rejected or transformed. The topic of the investigations became to understand this process, which thus became the topic of the "conversation." The central issue became how this classroom community, with the teacher as principal director, could recognize and affirm a child's own intentions and, at the same time, negotiate an entry for that child into mainstream discourse.

The maturing methodology, which the teachers used to explore their topic, tapped teachers' intuitive moments of puzzlement (what ethnographers might call "dissonant moments"), captured on the run through field notes, stories, and transcripts, and amplified in weekly meetings in which the data were discussed. These meetings were, at least initially, a central part of the methodology, for they provided teachers the "time" to stop time and the opportunity, through respectful critique, to understand an event and its meanings. From the beginning, group members intended to develop a new way of talking to each other that supported this new methodology.

The Turn

I define *turn* as the opportunity to speak. It is not intended, however, to be simply the opportunity to take the floor in a conversation, but rather the opportunity to speak in a bigger voice. The turns may vary in length and they may, through the local participants, bring in the virtual participants. All regularly meeting groups have some conventions for how turns operate.

The turn in the BTRS takes place over time, in a variety of formats—in small groups designed to give members an opportunity to present and have their data taken up by the group, or in whole-group meetings. Even though other members may comment at length when a member's data are presented, it is the presenting member's opportunity to have the group consider what has captured his/her deepest attention.

In the BTRS, what I call the turn may take place in a recursive process over a period of a year or even two. In the beginning of the turn, a member addresses the topic by bringing forth an embodiment of it: a transcript, a field note, a question, or a particularly striking story that evokes the question of children's intentions in the classroom community and teachers' understandings of them. But the turn does not end on that day because both the presenter and the group consider these phases of a turn as explorations, as opportunities to think and rethink, as an opportunity for the teacher to revisit the classroom in the company of colleagues. The turn does not end with a teacher's consideration of data: It often continues as members support and critique the development of written papers and presentations. This phase of the turn is an opportunity to theorize about the work. In fact, this feature of the turn in the BTRS requires that we think somewhat differently about who owns the turn. In the BTRS, the contributions of other members to a turn over months and years result in the turn being partially owned by the entire group, in a way that will become clear in the following description.

An example: "I need people stories." Steve Griffin has written in Chapter 2 about the content of this turn, which took over a year. I will discuss it here only as representative of what a turn is in the BTRS, and how a turn may develop over time.

Steve began this turn with a problem: David, a child in Steve's second-grade class, seemed to have broken the implicit rules of sharing time. Instead of telling a relatively short and factual story, David would begin by saying, "I've got a joke," and would then continue with an elaborate story. As this turn began, Steve simply related this as a story. Such stories often signaled the beginning of a larger investigation. The group considered it, but no implications were drawn, or conclusions reached. It was simply a moment of recognition, puzzlement, and delight for BTRS members, who often took great pleasure in hearing of these moments when a child "took the floor."

A few weeks later, Steve reported that he had "given in" to David's style and had begun to allow him to tell these stories at length. At that point, Steve brought data, the transcript of one of David's sharing-time episodes, to a meeting and directed several members in an oral reading. Through this activity the group became intimately aware of the activity in Steve's classroom around this moment. Steve wondered whether it was right to devote a great deal of time to David's stories, and whether it was right to allow lengthy turns that might interfere with the timely progression of the prescribed curriculum. Members commented at length on many aspects of David's story. Steve noted that the comments of the seminar members "allowed me to recognize that these stories represented real intellectual work on David's part and provided me with support and the courage to allow David to continue with his storytelling" (Griffin, 1993, p. 44). This gave Steve support to allow David to continue with his lengthy fictions, despite Steve's uncertainty about the meaning and value of this activity.

Months later, Steve continued his turn. He reported that David was not finished developing this genre, which had become an important part of the classroom's sharing time. Using field notes, Steve told the group about David's new variations. A few weeks later, Steve continued his turn by bringing in a lengthy transcript of one such episode. This is the genre that came to be known in his class and in the BTRS as "I need people stories."

In this turn, as in virtually all the others that have taken place over the years, the turn taker was unveiled, in the sense that he came to the group with a confusion that laid bare some aspect of teaching. He showed himself facing a dilemma, which he opened up to the group. The group's response, as Steve says, gave him courage both to pursue and explore his course in the classroom, and to take up the events as a topic for research within the group, to push it further as a systematic exploration, and eventually to write about it.

Without the group, Steve might not have been able to develop the idea of "I need people stories," which came to stand in the group for a child's ability to bring new genres of interaction into a classroom, genres that incorporate other members of the community. And without Steve's work on this, other teachers might not have seen as deeply into what their own students were capable of doing. For example, Karen Gallas (1994) found a child in her first-grade classroom who began, in quite a different way, to do the same thing as David.

The BTRS continues to consider classroom practice and interactions in the light of what Steve found in his turn. We are all still puzzling about the meaning of events in which children take over and transform the energy of a classroom community through a performance that involves a complex use of language. Steve's "I need people" turn, including his description and analysis of the events, has become an exemplar of what happens when one uncovers "a child's complex intentions" (Michaels, 1982, p. 442).

What Kind of Conversation Is Created Out Of These Turns?

Let us look at who has entered this conversation. One group of participants are the children whose voices are embodied in the transcripts. Children's voices are lifted out of the rush of classroom events and brought in as a focal point of attention among this group of teachers and researchers. Another participant, of course, is the teacher who leads the turn. He is present in the transcript as he works in the classroom and in his presentation of both the wonder and the pain that events of this sort evoke. Finally, teachers and researchers in the group use this turn not only to consider this particular dilemma, but also to expand their understanding of their own classrooms, and to expand their ability to look at language as it is enacted in the complex life of any classroom. Reciprocally, the turn taker gets to carry these voices back to his own classroom.

Note also the presence of other virtual participants in this turn—the curriculum planners of Steve's district. Although he has relative freedom in the way in which he implements the prescribed curriculum, the district prescribes a dense and tightly packed year of material. At every point, Steve's choices involve relinquishing either his own interests and judgment or those of the prescribed curriculum. Thus this voice, however muted by the group, is always present.

The academic researchers in the group are local participants and generally do not play the role of theorists. Rather, they play the role of the teacher members, generally rooting for the child's intentions and marveling at the complexity of the child's language and its ability to transform classroom interaction. There are theorists present, also, as virtual participants. Shirley Brice Heath, Jim Gee, Sarah Michaels, and Courtney Cazden all posed questions to the group through their writings about the ways that the complex intentions of children can be masked by cultural differences. The group posed a question back to them, a question about opening up the classroom to allow a space to examine the intentions and language in use, a question about the potential for change in the classroom.

What Other Conversations Were Entered?

Taken as a whole, the BTRS entered many conversations outside of the group's conversation through the channel of public presentations. These were of two types. One was presentations to groups of visitors and board members of the Literacies Institute, the funder of the BTRS for the first 4 years. After the first year, the teachers also presented in the form of papers, at a number of public forums, discussions of the data they had analyzed in the group. Among these were a group presentation to teachers and ethnographers at the University of Pennsylvania Ethnography in Education Forum, a group presentation at the American Educational Research Association (AERA), and a presentation at the Modern Language Association conference.

Numerous written works also came from members of the group, including Phillips and colleagues, 1993; Gallas, 1994, 1995; Ballenger, 1999; Swaim, 1998; and others. Both conference presentations and published papers are considered and supported in the weekly meetings.

CONCLUSION

This account of the BTRS is intended to help frame the following chapters for the reader. But it also has a political purpose. Public recognition of the essential and unique nature of teachers' knowledge has grown in recent years. Although there are increasingly numerous forums in which teachers can speak and write about their work, the knowledge of practice remains marginal in universities and public forums like the AERA annual meeting. I want to move this knowledge toward the center of the action and the conversation in academic and policy-making institutions. The BTRS is one example of a group that has forged a collaboration between teachers and academics that respects the teacher's voice. I hope that this analysis will provide a point of entry for similar collaborations.

Teachers have the responsibility to stay open to the particulars of their work. Similarly, researchers and policy makers also must stay open to the particulars of classrooms and schools. To do this, they need to attend to what teachers have to say when teachers create their own conversations. For this joining to happen, then, teachers must have their own conversations. They need to have the means to speak with one another, on their own terms. What are the conditions that permit this? What kinds of interactions give teachers a point of entry into a conversation outside the realm of their own classroom? I chose the metaphor of the conversation as part of an attempt to begin to answer this question.

I want to highlight a few features that we uncovered about the nature of a good conversation. It was necessary for us to open ourselves—our judgment, our practice—to public scrutiny. We found we could not consider a child or the child's learning apart from our interaction with that child. The other participants offered comments and questions that allowed each of us to hold the interaction up to a critical light and to reconsider and critique it. Other participants would not suggest changes in practice or critique the teacher's actions. Rather, we see the work in the group as a way for all the participants to revisit and expand the knowledge of teaching.

This is a different style of talk than that found in academic and policy-making institutions where people consider the practice of others. If someone has opened herself up to scrutiny in the way found here, she is not merely arguing about ideas. Therefore, careful consideration must be given to creating a way of talking that gives teachers the opportunity to revisit and re-examine their practice while sustaining the courage required to do this.

There are many unanswered questions. One important question is how to open conversations so that teachers and researchers can hear one another and, in turn, be heard by policy makers. Although all of these teachers act with skill and authority, they do so in the context of "an uncertain craft" (McDonald, 1992). The metaphor of a conversation, with its focus on voices, may allow us to reframe certain questions about teaching so that the answers we find and the questions we develop do not exclude those who do the work. Each chapter in this book is an exemplar of a turn in the larger conversation.

CHAPTER 2

I Need People: Storytelling in a Second-Grade Classroom

Steve Griffin

"I've got a joke," says David, a handsome, 7-year-old African-American boy. He smiles at his audience of classmates sitting on the floor before him, 2 months into their second-grade year. "Is it one of your long ones?" someone asks. "Yeah!" David replies. The audience shifts into more comfortable positions, settling in for a long story with obvious delight.

During this performance, I, the teacher, remain unsettled. The unspoken, but firmly rooted rules of sharing time have been toppled by a 7-year-old, and I'm not sure what I should do about it. Some of these rules, such as the appropriate length of a share and acceptable topics, were formed in the children's early years of schooling and came with them as they entered my second-grade classroom. Other rules were negotiated as this new class came into contact with my expectations and practices, for example, the acceptability of jokes as a topic for sharing time. I had agreed that we could share jokes. However, David's jokes did not fit into the category of jokes that I or his classmates expected.

I brought my discomfort to the BTRS. They responded with curiosity and great interest. My contact with the teachers and university researchers in the group helped me to recognize that David's jokes represented real intellectual work on his part, and provided me with the support and the courage to allow David to continue with his storytelling. This was fortunate for David, the rest of the children in the class, and me, as oral storytelling became a lively and important part of our curriculum for the rest of the year. This is the story of what I learned from David and his classmates.

SHARING TIME

Sharing time is a very common routine in many elementary classrooms. At first glance, it appears to be fairly simple and straightforward: Children take the sharing chair in front of the class and tell a story to their classmates, often an account of a family event or a sleepover with a friend or the demonstration of a new toy. Teachers shape it in various ways in order to reap the many potential benefits for the individual child and classroom culture. Sharing time may be one of the few times in a busy day when a child can choose a topic and create a fairly lengthy oral text on it (Cazden, 1988). And by listening to these stories, teachers can gain insights into the experiences and cultures of the children in their classroom that can provide guidelines for developing relevant curriculum (McCabe, 1997). The intermingling of individual children's stories during whole-class, sharing-time events creates a shared imaginative world specific to that classroom culture and to which each child has contributed as a storyteller and audience member (Dyson & Genishi, 1994). Through the act of telling a story or listening to the story of another, children acquire skills in crafting and listening to lengthy, complex, and interesting texts. In addition to the development of oral language abilities, these skills also carry over to facilitate the development of some reading and writing skills. It is for these reasons that oral storytelling has been a favorite classroom activity for me and the children in my classes throughout the years.

However, there are many features of sharing time that are both well accepted by participants and at the same time highly implicit. I was not the only one who recognized that, despite the storytelling expertise being displayed by David, certain rules about this well-routinized classroom event were being broken. In the beginning, David's attempts at jokes were met with many grumbles from the audience. The unwritten rule about length appeared to be "speak for less than 2 minutes," for at that point children began to look at me to intercede, many even mumbling, "When is he going to be done?"

The next few sharing times were begun with my stating that children could speak for as long as they wanted during sharing time. Eventually the children relaxed their view of the acceptable-length-of-share rule, and they began to look forward to David's jokes.

I present this excerpt from a story David told during this time, in order to provide the flavor of his stories. The story to this point has three girls following a mysterious old lady throughout a village, and uses lively rhythmic language to chronicle the movement of the children, such as in these lines:

> So they ran down the street
> Up the corner
> Past the railroad track
> Down the village
> Until they saw her again.

And later in the story:

> So they ran past the . . .
> Past the woods.
> They ran past the garden.
> Through the woods
> Back home.

David relates the first face-to-face meeting of the girls and the woman this way:

> They ran back to the village.
> And she (the old woman) was still there.
> Kate had a fish hook to get her by a mile.
> And so she threw it.
> And she turned into something.
> She turned into an eagle.
> Kelly screamed like nobody you ever heard before.
> She screamed so loud the earth began to shake.

All of David's stories were filled with similarly wonderful uses of language and imagery. His style was fueled by and organized around the delighted responses of his audience, who would laugh, boo, hiss, or respond verbally at appropriate points. Kate and Kelly were both characters in the story, as well as characters with the names of children in the classroom. David's technique of including the names of various children in the plots seemed to create a shared investment in the jokes and their outcomes. I wondered if by calling these "jokes," David was highlighting the importance of direct audience reaction to his stories, an important aspect of the telling of the kind of jokes I was used to.

As Christmas vacation approached, the class had developed a satisfying interactive rhythm during these stories, with David as storyteller (no other child had attempted to tell a story) and the audience as comfortable, involved, experienced respondent. We could have continued quite happily in this relationship for the rest of the year, but David wasn't finished developing the genre. He challenged the invisible conventions and pushed through unseen barriers again in a way that was the next obvious step, but that I would never have seen on my own.

I NEED PEOPLE

One day, after taking the sharing seat at the front of the room, David announced, "For this story I need people. Who wants to be in my story?" Before this, David had used some unwritten yet democratic method for choosing classmates to be characters in his stories. Since children often begged him to be included, I assumed that, when David said he needed people, he was just being more visible about this process of choosing characters. I thought he wanted them to escalate their bids for inclusion. But he had something different in mind. The children he chose, two boys and a girl, were instructed to stand and act out his story. As David told the story, his chosen peers performed it for the whole class. This served to accentuate the issues of anger, humor, and other emotions expressed in the story. In addition, it elevated the audience response and engagement to a new level.

As an example, David told the following story in January, soon after he had transformed his storytelling into a participatory activity. After spending several minutes choosing his actors and giving them brief stage directions, he began his story.

> *David:* Once upon a time there lived a royal prince. He liked his
> palace . . . castle. One day another prince, . . . well, Bill's the
> prince.
> *Bill:* Well, where should I go?
> *David:* Anywhere. Then the prince had come and seen what his
> royal palace was like. And then another . . . another. . . .
> There was a king who came. . . . He had a great . . . he had a
> great king hat. And he always weared boots . . . every single
> day. And there was another boy. There was a little boy who
> . . . who had . . . who never, who didn't have a family. The
> prince had came out. . . . The prince came out and said to

the boy, "Well, are you hun . . . do you have a father and
mother?" And the boy . . . the little boy said no. . . . And then
all of a sudden this horse . . . this horse trotted along. (Jason,
playing the horse, crawls on all fours and makes loud horse
sounds.) The horse was very excited. Because today was his
birthday. He always [unintelligible] (Lots of noise from Jason.
David is hard to hear.) And the royal prince said to him,
"Heel boy heel." And Ja . . . and the horse stopped. Like a
thousand dollar bills. Like a cannon ball. The horse was very
un. . . . This was very bad for the horse. The prince was put
on punishment by the kind, by his, the prince's father. One
day a prince came. She had polka dots on.

Child: Princess, you mean.

David: And she always weared polka dots because she liked
polka dots a lot. The horse was very excited to see her. (lots
of horse noises from Jason) He went over to her and pre-
tended like he was a dog. (Jason makes horse noises.)

Girl: You're acting like a dog, horse.

Jason: Thank you.

David: And the horse stops. (loudly) And he flabbergas, he was
flabbergasted! Another prince came. She had—wow—you
could talk about her! She had some wild pants on. (lots of
laughter) I mean talking real wild. And Duncan, the king,
Duncan, he was the one who had brown [unintelligible]. He
said to her, "Well young lady. What's your name?" And the
prince said, "I don't got no name." (said with speed and
weird intonation) (lots of laughing and talking in audience)
And the horse said, "She gots a name. (again, with strange
intonation) Her name is Philadelphia." (lots of laughing
and talking) And then along came a big, big . . . big, I mean
talking some big time . . . giant. (more laughing) Jason the
horse was so afraid he ran, he went galloping away. (scared
horse noises) Like a runaway hamster. (Jason makes more
noise, runs around wildly.) Stop. Cut. Cut it.

Jason: Daniel who was . . . very the brave person . . . to fight this
king . . . to fight this dragon. He had a sword. But he didn't
fight with the sword. He fights with words.

Daniel: Hallelujah. (points fingers at girl playing the giant/
dragon; lots of laughing)

David: He said hallelujah every time to the giant. The giant got
bored and said, OK, OK come on come on. Stop this non-

> sense. (Daniel continues to repeat hallelujah.) And then the prince, the knight stopped the nonsense. So along came her brother. He was so big. Hey dude, what's up? Bill, you're not the giant.
>
> *Bill:* I'm not?
>
> *David:* He was actor Daniel. (Lots of commotion. David's narration hard to hear. Some sort of fighting is going on.) Then the giant had no more brothers. The End.

Although the story is somewhat difficult to follow from the transcript, it was coherent and very much appreciated when actually presented to the audience of second graders. "I need people" stories became an immediate hit, but they remained a genre unique to David. His classmates continued to describe a weekend trip, discuss an upcoming slumber party, or talk about other real-life events in routine ways when it was their turn to share.

I was curious to know what other children would do with this genre, or whether other genres might develop if other children felt free to produce fictional narratives during sharing time. In the middle of January, I announced that we were no longer having sharing time, but storytelling time. Children could tell any kind of story they wanted, true or made-up, in any way they liked. Sharing time immediately changed. Although some children continued to tell narratives of real-life events, most began to tell fictional stories. Some told what we called "sit and tells," where the storyteller tells a story to an audience seated before the child. However, most children told "I need people" stories, with classmates performing the story as it was told. This genre was always signified by the child taking possession of the sharing chair at the front of the room and announcing, "I need people." By the end of the year, David's classmates became experienced "I need people" storytellers, with almost every child in the class, including the children who rarely spoke voluntarily, producing one of these stories at some point during the second half of the year.

David, however, remained the master. He developed a style that was theatrically and linguistically engaging. He played with multisyllabic words, often taken from our curriculum, and made them seem new and delightful. For instance:

"And the horse stops. He was flabbergasted!"

"And her name is . . . Philadelphia."

He also created imaginative similes, often making connections between events in his stories and classroom events. For example:

> "And the horse stopped . . . like a thousand dollar bill like a cannon ball."

> "And the horse was was so afraid he ran . . . he went galloping away . . . like a runaway hamster." [The classroom hamster had recently escaped.]

He also creatively integrated content from our classroom curriculum into his stories, demonstrating a deep understanding of that content. For instance, the story printed earlier was told just after a unit on Dr. Martin Luther King and included the following lines:

> "Daniel who was very . . . the brave person . . . to fight this king . . . to fight this dragon. He had a sword. But he didn't fight with the sword. He fights with words."

LEARNING FROM STORIES

David's ability to integrate aspects of school, home, and familiar literature into his stories was highly developed, reflecting a depth of understanding that other school activities did not highlight. With time, the other children began incorporating some of these stylistic devices into their oral and written stories as well, and their stories became much richer and more complex as a result. The rest of the class members were improving their linguistic and narrative skills thanks to David. But they also were contributing to David's acquisition of other ways of telling stories, ways that were important to school success.

David's stories were very loosely constructed. Events did not necessarily follow one from the other, characters would be introduced and then never mentioned again, and some problems might be established but never resolved. It may be that the looseness of his narrative structure was necessary to allow the imagery, metaphor, and linguistic play to come to the forefront in his storytelling. But a tighter form of narrative construction would be required in many future school activities, and David had not yet displayed an ability to produce this kind of story, even though I had attempted to help him develop tighter story construction during our individual writing conferences. However, many of the other children in the class were producing stories with a more central organization to their plot, and David was not only hearing this type of story organization from them, but also acting in the stories.

Many of his classmates' stories related to an issue that apparently was very important to these children, that of gender relationships. Can boys and girls play together? Are there activities that are only for boys or only for girls? These were important concerns for these children, and these themes continued to arise in their "I need people" stories until the theme almost became a cliche. The movement in narrative form and in content development that characterized the week-to-week progression of the "I need people" form seemed to become stuck. David helped bring closure to this line of story when he one day produced a marvelously tight, carefully crafted story in which the boys end up playing Barbies for the rest of their lives and the girls are left playing Nintendo forever. He apparently had become impatient with the gender relationship theme, and he cleverly resolved it by deftly using the more tightly constructed narrative genre that many of the other children regularly used.

David's "gender story," told in March, on a day when torrential rains had created a flood in our classroom, follows:

> *David:* Once, there was three girls named Jamie, Jessica, and Joanna. One day, they went over to the boys' house. Who is there, you little rats? And they said, Me, just us. And the girls said, Okay, will you let us in? And they said, Why? Because we don't want rain coming in this house. We don't want any rain coming in this house. And the girls went back to their house. And they played Barbies. (laughter) So they went over the boys' house one last time. And it was [unintelligible] ing [unintelligible] too. And knocked on the door. And they said, Who's there? They said, Can you let us in? And the boys said, Yes. And the boys stayed at the girls' house for the rest of their lives.
> *Children:* Playing Barbies?
> *David:* Playing Barbies. (lots more laughter)

By developing ability in another style, which was more centrally organized, David was again regaining control of the themes and style of the storytelling experience. But the result was also that David was guided into learning a more mainstream, school-based way of narration, one that he had found difficult to acquire in the context of the typical school curriculum.

CONCLUSION

David is a gifted and persistent storyteller, who most likely would have found some other way to make his stories heard if I had thwarted his attempts to manipulate sharing time to meet his needs. But what about the other children's powerful voices that are yet to be heard because there is no existing public space for their yet unknown way of making sense and reasoning? I thought that I had created a classroom that would encourage these myriad ways of making sense. But after watching David persistently pursue a new genre of storytelling for this classroom, pushing through unwritten rules and constraints, I realized that the type of talk that was allowed in the classroom was constrained in ways invisible to me as the teacher. What other constraints are operating in my classroom that are still unknown to me, effectively inhibiting children's full use of their endowment of language and reasoning skills? My work as a teacher must include developing my receptivity to the countless ways that children think and express their sense making to others. I can't know how all children talk, or how they think, because in listing the ways I think they do this, I immediately exclude the ways that are not on my list. Instead, I need to develop structures and an openness that somehow will allow these different ways to appear, and to feel welcomed in the classroom, which should result in a richer experience for all the children.

CHAPTER 3

Reading Storybooks
with Young Children:
The Case of *The Three Robbers*

CYNTHIA BALLENGER

When I read a storybook to my preschool students, like most teachers of young children, I talk about the book with them as well as read the text. I do this both after the book is finished and sometimes while we are reading the story. I believe that talking with them keeps the children interested and engaged. More important, I believe that this talk helps them to connect with the book by relating it to experiences in their own lives.

Cochran-Smith in *The Making of a Reader* (1984) explains the kind of talk I mean; she characterizes the talk that teachers value in these situations as talk that involves a sort of mental movement from the child's life to the experiences depicted in the text. For example, I might ask a question like, "Do you have a doggie at your house?" as I am reading a book about dogs. The child is then expected to think of his or her own dog, or to think of people who have a dog, and to use knowledge of this familiar situation to make sense of the book. The children learn to bring whatever relevant experience they have and connect it to the book's topic.

I have been told that I read stories well. I think about which books we should read and what activities we might do with them, but I rarely worry about how we should talk about the books as we read. The kinds of questions I ask, the remarks I make, seem almost natural to me, as a teacher, as a devoted reader myself and as a parent. I expect the children to imaginatively and emotionally enter the book, to rejoice when the story leads that way, to worry or grieve when it is sad, and to care about the story and the characters.

In this chapter I want to describe an experience of teaching where I found I did have to worry about storybook reading and talk. In this experience, I encountered ways of talking about books that were unfamiliar to me. The children didn't do what I expected, and because they didn't, and because I couldn't easily teach them to, I was forced to reconsider and to question my practice of storybook reading.

MY CONCERNS

I taught for 3 years in an early childhood classroom of Haitian children. The children were 4- and 5-year-olds, and many of them were born in Haiti. Some were born here of immigrant parents. Their parents all spoke Haitian Creole. Since I also speak Haitian Creole fairly well, although not perfectly, we used both English and Creole in this classroom.

I knew that these children did not regularly hear bedtime stories at home. I also knew that the bedtime story plays an important part in preparing children for the tasks of school literacy (Heath, 1983). I hoped to help my students to become familiar with books and to love them as I did.

The Three Robbers by Tomi Ungerer (1991) was the book that the children loved above all others. From the first day we read it, they talked about it, pored over the pictures pretending to read, and carried it around with them during the school day. I could see clearly that it was important to them. And yet it was a long time before we ever managed to finish it. As I read, they would constantly interrupt. The discussion would go far afield and although I tried to bring us back to the book, I rarely succeeded. The children were too excited, too interested in what they were talking about.

I brought my problem to the BTRS. I was frustrated. I explained to my colleagues that the children didn't know how to listen to storybooks. They were so excited when I read to them that they just talked and the book was forgotten. The response I received was an example of one of the important practices of the seminar. Rather than trying to help me fix this situation, to teach the children to listen better, they wanted to know what was going on. Before we tried to fix anything, we needed to know, and to reflect on, what the children were saying and doing. The rest of this chapter is an account of what we learned from this.

TALK AROUND BOOKS: MY STUDENTS' VIEW

The following conversation is taken from the transcript of the very first time we read *The Three Robbers*. Text from the book is italicized. Text in parentheses is translation of what was said in Haitian Creole, and I have used Xs to indicate unintelligible speech. The material in brackets gives additional useful information.

Eveline: Three robbers, I'm three, I'm three, I'm three.

Cindy: Yeah, 1,2,3. be quiet sit down. Si ou ta vle tande, pa pale, OK? (If you would like to hear, don't talk, OK?) It says the three robbers [pointing at title]. *Once upon a time there were three fierce robbers. They went about hidden under large black capes and tall black hats.*

Jean: One eye XX only one.

Cindy: Yeah, it looks like he's only got one eye he's got his hat down here.

Jean: Only two eyes XX [evidently referring to himself].

Cindy: Yeah, I think this guy has probably got two eyes but his hat is down. You know he's hiding so nobody knows who he is cuz he's bad.

Jean: Why?

Jeanson: Bad guy!!!

Cindy: *The first had a blunderbuss.* You see this kind of a gun.

Jean: Gun gun.

Cindy: *The second had a pepper-blower,* you see that? It puts piman in people's eyes, you see that, pepper.

Jean: Pepper?

Cindy: Yeah, pepper, it's piman.

Jeanson: My daddy eat piman. I eat piman.

Cindy: You eat piman too?

Tayla: My daddy eat piman.

Jean: Everybody eat piman.

Cindy: Do you like it in your eyes?

Many children: Daddy piman. I like it. No. Food. Daddy. Mommy. Not my brother.

Cindy: But in your eyes?

Jean: No. No eyes.

Tayla: Cindy, I eat in my eyes [laughing].

Kenthea: I drink my medicine myself. Cindy, I drink my medicine. My mother take medicine too.

Suzanne: My mother give me my medicine, green medicine.

The children are initiating all the talk here and they are talking to each other. They're building on one another's remarks. They're having a wonderful time. To me, however, they seem to be ignoring the book, and I try to bring their attention back to it. I find myself holding up the book to the children's view as if I thought they had forgotten it, or me.

With the help of conversation in the seminar, I began to explore this conversation. I found that I recognized more than one of the children's seemingly random remarks from other moments in the school day. Eveline responds to the word *three* in the title, *The Three Robbers*: "I'm three, I'm three, I'm three." She is 3 and she will fight anyone who believes that he or she is also 3. She greets the number, not by exploring its role in the text, but by saying something important about herself with it.

Jean contrasts his situation with the robber's—the robber has only one eye (or so it appears from the picture), while Jean has two. In fact, Jean's reference to eyes is a recurring theme in his play and conversation. A few days before we read *The Three Robbers* he had told a story about throwing sugar in a dog's eyes. His interest in eyes and maybe in his body's symmetry reapppears a few days later when he is finding a partner to walk outside with.

> *Jean:* Cindy, hold my hand?
> *Cindy:* I only have two hands, Jean [both are already being held].
> *Jean:* Two hands, two eyes, one mouth [with evident satisfaction].

Jean remains concerned with aspects of this issue throughout the year; the final appearance I note is in a version of *Jack and the Beanstalk* that he dictated near the end of the year.

> Once upon a time there was zombie.
> Zombie no wanta eat Jack.
> Jack want some food.
> And big giant in the house.
> Mother say, "No, big giant in the house and big zombie."
> Jack have a rock.
> Jack throw the rock in the zombie's eyes and zombie's eye get
>   out.
> Only one eye stay.

Neither eyes nor the number 3 is a main theme of *The Three Robbers*. Eveline and Jean do not appear to be moving from their experience back to the text, as Cochran-Smith suggests they should. And yet, even though Eveline presumably already knows her age, and Jean the number of his eyes, one senses a great force behind their statements. These are the sorts of comments that teachers of young children puzzle over all the time—statements of completely obvious facts, made with enormous conviction and pride.

The discussion about piman (pepper) has a similar feeling of engaged and excited public pronouncement. In the book, pepper is sprayed into the eyes of horses that are pulling a stagecoach to make them stop. Then the robbers rob the passengers of the stagecoach. But in their conversation, the children are talking about something else, something they are coming to know further as they speak. This is the meaning of pepper in Haitian culture. Piman is an important spice in Haitian cooking. An adult Haitian is expected to eat food with piman, hot food; for children, however, the piman often is left out. When I serve the children unfamiliar food, they often question me, "Pa gen piman?" (It doesn't have piman?) before they are willing to taste it.

Jean introduces the theme, "My daddy eat piman." Tayla seconds this. Jean then makes the generalization, "Everybody eat piman." I intervene, in typical teacher fashion, by asking them to connect their discussion with the story line, "Do you like it in your eyes?" I was concerned with bringing the discussion back to the book. This sort of remark, in many classrooms where I have taught, would have brought the children right back to the book. Here, after Jean answers me, the children all together and with great enthusiasm summarize their experience of piman. From what I can understand of that segment, they are mentioning various people who eat piman and others who don't. Then Tayla says, "Cindy, I eat in my eyes," and laughs as she says this; I believe she was making a joke by joining my focus, "pepper in the eyes" with theirs, "eating." Finally Kenthea brings up her ability, and her mother's, to take medicine by herself, a point that Suzanne seconds.

The children were identifying the place of piman in their world and in their fathers' world. Piman is for adults. It is a sign of maturity. In their view it is particularly fathers who like the very hot food, so pepper is a sign of masculinity. Perhaps it was no coincidence that it was two girls, Kenthea and Suzanne, who brought up medicine. I believe they were making an analogy between taking medicine and eating piman. Both piman and medicine are signs of power. Mothers are the ones who handle medicine, and fathers are able to eat piman. Through this conversation the children have begun to interpret, for themselves and for me, the meaning of piman in their families and their culture. They are helping me know them, and discovering something for themselves as well.

However, their interpretation of the role of piman in Haitian culture is not a part of the story of *The Three Robbers*. The book is not the center of this conversation. The children are aware of the book in various ways, but they are focusing on issues situated in their world. In Cochran-Smith's terms, they are not moving from life to text, but the other way. Nor am I the center. They are talking to each other. This conversation, like so many others I experienced that year, left me feeling rather out of control and frustrated, and yet impressed with the children and their lively engagement. The children themselves seemed enormously pleased with what they had done.

TALK AROUND BOOKS—MY COMMUNITY'S VIEW

I was afraid we would never come to understand the book. How would they manage in first grade? I was nevertheless impressed with their seriousness, and I think it was this that led me to my next step—exploring the conversations I had with my friends when we talked about books. I listened carefully to what people said whenever a book was mentioned. What I found was not what I expected. I found that the practice of literate adults, even teachers, when they were talking about books outside of school, was not the same as the practice of the same people in school. It was, in fact, more similar to the way my students incorporated the book as part of a larger conversation. When the people I listened to brought up a book in conversation, comprehending the book was rarely the goal that organized the conversation; the book was discussed in relation to its usefulness in the task of understanding important aspects of life. A book that contained a terminally ill character, for example, led to a recounting of experiences in this area. A book that contained a divorce, led to a discussion of divorce. We would take events or characters from the book and use them in the arguments and stories we were developing on our own topics, as the children did around "piman" or eyes. And this happened whether or not these situations were part of the central themes of the book.

I was recently in a conversation about a book in which two of the characters were cousins. The conversation turned to recollections of various kinds of trouble the participants had gotten into as children with their cousins and then to speculations as to why cousins appeared to get into more trouble together in childhood than nonrelations. One of us, a very responsible adult, had gotten into significant trouble with his cousins as a child, and the conversation was a serious one as he tried to understand himself as a child. And yet this was not a central theme of the book. The goal of this adult discussion was not to comprehend the book, but rather to use the book to understand ourselves. We used the book to address concerns of our own. And yet, the book changed through these conversations. It gained more life from the context of these concerns. I told a cousin story or two to this group of friends, as each of us did, and now, when I return to this book, I think of it as another cousin story. That the author made the two characters cousins now has more resonance for me, literary resonance and resonance from real life.

THE SOURCES OF INTERPRETATION

But is that all we do? Can we follow our own lead and the vagaries of our connections and still end up understanding the book as written? As I listened and thought about my own ways of reading, I realized that it isn't only that we wrest control from the book and go our own way. We also, as we read, let the book take us places we haven't been, didn't know about, couldn't have gone without it. In this case we read in order to incorporate the imagined experience of the novel into our own experiences, to make sense of people and events with the help of experiences we've gained from books, to learn about people we otherwise might not know. So, for example, someone reads a memoir of the childhood of a very rich boy and realizes something of the loneliness of her husband, whose background was similar. A novel that includes a very religious character helps a reader who lives a very secular life to understand something of the character of religion.

Were my students using literature to imagine experiences they had not had and were unfamiliar with? Were they willing to let the book lead them places they hadn't been? I was very concerned about these questions since I was afraid that the answer was no. My students, it seemed to me, refused to give up control to the book. Not only did they travel far afield in their discussions of books, but they actually on occasion refused to believe the text as written. Listen to Giles, for example.

Giles was perhaps a little narrow in what he considered worthy themes for literature. He preferred that all stories include a mother, and his idea of a plot usually revolved around danger to the mother. His own mother was about to have a new baby and perhaps Giles was placing some of his own worries into the literature we read. Here he proposed a way to make sure that his theme was included in *The Tortoise and the Hare*. I was almost to the end of the book when I closed it in order to respond to a discussion about whether we had school the following day. Giles then took over:

> *Giles:* Cindy, Cindy, lemme talk.
> *Cindy:* OK, let's listen to Giles.
> *Giles:* Open da book [I open it to our current page, a picture of the hare, which we are calling a rabbit].
> *Giles:* [staring into the book] The rabbit mommy's dead. The bad guy get knife and he XX. Another one rabbit get a knife [I start to close the book while listening to him]. Open da book [I reopen the book] and the bad guy rabbit XXXXXX.

This was only one of several times that Giles attempted to include in my reading a piece of plot involving the death of a mother. This time, however, he was particularly insistent that the book be open as he told his part of the story, and as he did so, he stared fixedly at the book as if he were finding something in there.

Like the others, he seemed to find in literature a context for considering the themes that absorbed him in the rest of his life. If the story did not speak to his concern, Giles was willing to insert his concern among the book's characters. I was concerned that he did not understand the role of print in reading. He seemed to think that I simply was making up words to say as I read, just as he did.

My concern in this regard was strengthened by the students' unwillingness to accept the ending of *The Three Robbers* as written. In the book three robbers rob stagecoaches; they use a pepper-blower to blow pepper into the horses' eyes, a blunderbuss to scare the passengers, and an axe to chop up the stagecoaches' wheels. Then they steal the passengers' money and jewels. However, one night there are no rich passengers to plunder. The only one in the coach is an orphan named Tiffany who is going to live with a wicked aunt. The robbers decide to take her back to their cave where they put her cozily to bed. The next morning when she wakes up, she sees all their treasure. She asks them what the treasure is for. The robbers evidently had never realized that there might be a purpose for all their wealth. They quickly decide to set up a home for all the lost and abandoned children in the world and they become "kind foster fathers." This was the plot as I understood it. My students, however, did not accept the idea that the robbers had become good. The book's authority was not sufficient. My authority was not sufficient. Robbers are bad and they don't change, the students said.

Did they think they could change what was written? How could I help them understand how text really worked? We read the book over and over, and I did tell them frequently that the robbers had become good. I would tell them that the book said so and point to the print. I felt bound to convey to them the authority of the text. They, however, had gone to work finding what they needed in order to understand me and it was nothing I would have known to provide.

The concerted effort they put into making sense of our disagreement probably began with their interest in bad people. They became very focused on "bad" people. One book, in which a peripheral character is put in jail, was known as "the bad guy book," despite the book's main theme having to do with a lost apple. Another book, *The Red Balloon*, which contained bad boys, was called "the bad boy book." Whenever we read storybooks, the children were eager to identify all the bad characters. Jérémie and Paul were as serious as the others in their condemnation of bad behavior by trolls and wolves and boys. But I also began to notice that they regularly queried me about my belief that the robbers were not bad. I noted Jérémie's interest in my field notes.

> 4/91: Jérémie requesting a particular picture in *The Three Robbers*, identifies it as "when they change. Three robbers was going to be bad boys. Now they change."
>
> 5/91: Jérémie asking and asking how the three robbers changed. I could not really understand what he was getting at, but he was very persistent.

There followed a number of intense conversations whose significance I did not see at the time. I remembered them only because they were so odd. Jérémie showed me a paper towel that had been sharing his pocket with a leaky marker. The napkin had ink all over it. He told me over and over that it had changed. Another day he had something to tell me about a remote control and how it changed channels. Again I never quite understood him but he was very intense. He came to me with ice melting in his hand—and again said it was changing.

I understood what he had been concerned about only when I overheard the following conversation among Jérémie, Paul, and Giles. The boys were looking at *The Three Robbers* and Giles was trying to insert one of his usual episodes about mommys in it.

> *Giles:* And the robbers get this kid and the robbers get this mommy and they put them in the house.
> *Jérémie:* No, no.
> *Paul:* The robbers not gonna get her.
> *Jérémie:* Now the robbers is nice.

In this case Jérémie and Paul didn't allow Giles to use the text as the setting for the conversation he wanted to have. And they knew why— the robbers were now nice. How did they get there? And why was it so hard? I asked a number of American 3- and 4-year-olds what they thought of the robbers at the end of the book. Even the 3-year-olds knew that the robbers had changed and become good and could point at the picture where it happened. The 4-year-olds could explain why. American children evidently are brought up with a view of psychology as malleable and as open to events and environment. Bad behavior does not indicate bad character forever. Innocence and love, as represented by the orphan Tiffany, can change anything. These children recognized this plot and it fit with their view of the world.

Haitian children acquire a different philosophy. While children's mischief is actually both expected and tolerated quite easily, there is nevertheless an articulated belief that a child can be born bad, that some people are, and that there is not much one can do about it. It is much less common among Haitians than among Americans to hear explanations for why someone is bad. Haitian children hear fewer discussions regarding what the malefactor might have lacked, perhaps love or friendship, that would have helped him/her to act better. The more typical Haitian view is that one is supposed to act right whatever the circumstances. Character is not seen so readily as a product of the environment, not regarded as something that might change given different circumstances.

Jérémie and Paul, who probably had heard occasionally that their behavior was less than perfect, wanted to explore evil and to imagine what latitude there might be for ethical transformation. Perhaps it was interest in this issue that caused so many of the children to be deeply involved with this book. Jérémie focused on the way I was using the word *change*—he compared numerous versions of it. *The Three Robbers* offered him an experience he had not had with *change* and he wanted to understand it. Somehow he managed, by his various investigations of the word and what it meant, to imagine the kind of change exemplified in *The Three Robbers*. He was able to imagine that the three robbers were no longer bad by means of his talk about the stained paper towel, the melting ice, and the channel changer, and by looking at the picture in the book "where they changed." Perhaps he was making sure, by looking at the picture, that the robbers didn't change physically. I don't know. The way Jérémie used the resources at hand to make sense of the book, of my insistence, and of his various experiences is not something I could have orchestrated. My role in this was played out over time in these odd conversations with him and some of the other children, in which I certainly did not know that we were discussing change in relation to moral development.

The children's response contrasts with an experience I had with a friend, a highly literate adult. I had just finished re-reading *The Brothers Karamazov* by Dostoyevsky. I had asked my friend to read it too, and she had begun, but put it down. I asked her why. She said, "Well, couldn't he just lighten up." The characters in Dostoyevsky are often overwrought by today's standards. They are always full of tears and regularly throw themselves at the feet of one person or another. It takes an imaginative leap to enter that world—it's not the way we see the world today. My friend didn't, at least at that point, have the drive that Jérémie and Paul had, the drive to imagine a foreign world and to enter it.

Had they allowed the text to take them somewhere they had never been before? Had they traveled with a book into new territory? Certainly, but their way of managing this had not been one I had seen before. My experience with literature and with helping children engage with it had not included the approach these children took to comprehending and interpreting the book. Looking at how far afield Jérémie went, it seems very likely to me that all the conversations about piman and about eyes and about bad guys and bad boys and mothers in other books were in fact crucial for the work these children did on whether robbers could become good. Talking about their knowledge of pepper provided a way to join this story with their own stories. It allowed a connection, which paved the way for others. The conversations I had with my friends about cousins functioned in a similar way. What appears off-topic may in fact add to the set of connections out of which the full meaning and a full response arise. My original sense of the kinds of questions to ask in order to help children engage with a story seems quite impoverished compared with what these children thought to do to bring storybooks into the stories of their lives.

Before ending, let us return one final time to Jérémie, who, despite initial reluctance, showed as the year progressed more and more interest in promoting the book's role in the conversation. By the spring, he frequently wanted to know what the book said. If the discussion had taken off, and I was silent, he would ask the other children to stop talking so we could find out. However, in the text below we see that he and his classmates nevertheless did not desert their accustomed style of participation. Their remarks formed a tapestry of connections from other moments of the day. I was again reading the *Tortoise and the Hare* when the children began to comment:

> *Jean:* Rabbit bumped his head.
> *Jérémie:* And camel has a ugly face.
> *Giles:* And rabbit have a big big ear.
> *Emmanuel:* Gade, li gen bel soulye (Look, he has beautiful
>   shoes).
> *Jérémie:* Cindy's turn.

Jérémie first included the word *ugly*, with which he was fascinated for a period of time, "Camel has a ugly face." We had been to the zoo and he had heard the camel called ugly. *Ugly* often is used in Jérémie's community to describe nasty behavior. For example, a sullen child may be called *ugly*, and perhaps Jérémie had heard this addressed to himself. Jérémie knew, in addition, that in my dialect it could describe things that were not beautiful—a camel's face certainly qualified. He had been investigating the meanings of *ugly* in various contexts with his usual persistence. He had made this remark about the camel's face several times before. The other children each add their remarks, each perhaps part of a comparable inquiry. Jérémie then returned them to me, the reader, and the text. Although the book had gained a larger role in the conversation in the last two examples, book reading remained the setting for exploring a variety of important issues. Jérémie and the others had not abandoned their earlier view of the value of books and book reading, but they had added to it.

Do I know how to teach literature now? Have I better ideas about how to discuss storybooks? Rather than a revised plan or a new set of objectives, I now have a more elaborated narrative of classroom life with books. My classroom story now includes these children and their view of books. Including them has opened up my own assumptions for scrutiny and thus deepened immeasurably my own ability to think about literature and stories and their uses. The base from which I respond as children talk about literature is made more conscious by experiences such as these. Furthermore, and perhaps most important, by looking closely at what the children are doing in this sort of situation where they are fully engaged, I have enormous respect for their thinking and the seriousness of their approach to schooling.

CHAPTER 4

Students Talking and Writing Their Way into "Functional" Worlds

CINDY BESELER

As we walked down the street to [the hospital], the kids made a "Cindy sandwich" on either side of me. They do not do that at school. Rebecca leaned on my shoulder and teased me by pretending to push me into lampposts. They would not do that to a teacher at school. The guys tried to follow suit and I reacted differently to a male hanging on my shoulder. They learned a very valuable lesson that they could not have tested out at school. [At the same time] I felt very unprofessional. I know I'm respectfully honoring a very important kind of learning that develops only in private spaces. I just wonder if I'm not disrupting their learning in the public space.

I was accompanying four adolescents with special needs to their volunteer job during school hours when they made this "Cindy sandwich." Upon reflection, I began to see this as more than simply a physical act in an observational field note; it became a metaphor for how I repeatedly felt sandwiched between the different roles of "teacher." Over the past 10 years in the BTRS, I have examined what it means to be a teacher, to teach, to be a learner with special needs, and for students to learn from me as their teacher. I often have wondered how close to get to the students and how much distance to keep. Is it appropriate for me as a teacher to dismantle the power differential and use the role of friend or equal? Specifically, I wondered how much to get involved in oral or written conversations to model "appropriate communication" and how much to let the students talk or write without correction. Is stepping back to let students engage in unedited talking or writing still "teaching"?

These questions surface in mainstream classrooms as well, but are complicated in a special education class by the special abilities and disabilities of students. In such classrooms, the language and behavior of social roles such as friend, stranger, worker, acquaintance, and so on, must be explicitly taught. Teaching the students exclusively from a "teacher" script models only the forms of interaction required by the student role, and does not serve the students very well in the community where nonschool situations require different kinds of interactions. Without explicit instruction about the personal and social boundaries that prescribe how to relate to particular people in specific situations, the students naturally talked and acted from an overly open, personal stance. Once, a student started revealing details to a stranger on the bus about her period, not recognizing the listener's discomfort. Another student walked through hospital halls trying to give high-fives to unfamiliar doctors he felt respect for, and he greeted similarly unknown high-ranking bank executives by patting them on the shoulder and asking how their day was. Occasionally, he went into their offices to play with objects on their desks. He didn't consider asking for permission as he was taught to do in other circumstances, nor suspect that asking for that type of permission in this case would not be appropriate.

The need to teach explicit language use in particular contexts arises because of two sets of assumptions that are widely held: Students with language-based disabilities (1) are concrete and egocentric thinkers who do not generalize their thinking beyond the specific context, and (2) need to be taught a functional curriculum, that is, life skills that are meaningful to their daily lives. As I examined these assumptions, I realized that my sandwich metaphor is not only the private story of a reflective practitioner who feels a tension between varying roles. The assumptions also result in perpetuating the students' feelings of being sandwiched between different expected ways of being in the world, so this is their story too. I came to understand how the students must have felt the tug-of-war between their need to communicate with me and each other in their own natural ways and the need that I, as their teacher, imposed on them to learn to communicate in the particular ways of the nondisabled world. Ultimately, I knew I would have to dismantle the tensions I've described and let the students talk and write in ways that empowered them personally.

A TEACHER LEARNING ABOUT TALK

I began talking about the ethnographic details of my classroom to the BTRS by giving an abbreviated overview of who the students were, so that I wouldn't spend the whole hour at that impersonal level of describing their special needs. After all, when I listened to my BTRS colleagues give context about their elementary school students, I quickly was able to get a good general understanding of whom they were talking about. I realized that talking about special needs students is very different than talking about regular education students. The BTRS would not accept my casual abbreviated descriptions of my students, and they urged me to question the way I talked about them. With careful, repeated reflection, the descriptions have become important data in my teacher research work.

The automatic descriptions I gave of my students would be familiar to all special needs teachers who attempt in casual conversation to explain with few words a topic that needs a long explanation. The conversations often start like this: "What do you do?" I answer, "I am a teacher." "So, what do you teach?" A knot in my stomach grows as I feel the conversation's direction. "I teach high school students with disabilities." Inevitably, I get a response along the lines of, "Wow, you must have a lot of patience!" That feels misguided and lacking in respect for the very complex job I have and I refute it: "Not really, because I love what I'm doing" (which is true). "What kind of disabilities do they have, exactly?" "They have developmental delays," I answer and, knowing that they want me to tell them something less euphemistic, add, "they're mentally retarded." Usually this rouses an increased and again misplaced sympathy: "God bless you, those poor kids, they need someone like you." Awkward pause. "What are they capable of learning?" Another awkward pause.

This is the interesting point in the conversation because I know they're fishing to understand, to really figure out what the kids are like, what they can or cannot do. They need me to tap into any mental picture they might have, whether it is a drooling child in a wheelchair, or TV's Corky with Down's Syndrome from *Life Goes On*. Since personal descriptions such as "Rebecca likes the Beatles, and Arnold likes hieroglyphics," don't satisfy this need, at this point I used to blurt out a litany of general information much as I would write on a student's individual educational plan (IEP). This is where I unknowingly create a kind of Cindy sandwich by dishonoring how I really want to describe the students: "Well, they are concrete, egocentric thinkers and have trouble generalizing information. Many of them have receptive and expressive language difficulties and require a lot of repetition, with tasks broken down into small steps." This is a shorthand all special education teachers know, but is usually too obscure for nonteachers, and they continue, "What do you teach them?" I explain: "We especially spend a lot of time practicing social and communication skills. I teach them functional things—like grocery shopping, banking, riding public transportation, doing laundry, cooking—whatever skills they need to function as happily and independently as possible in community-based jobs."

My Students

I was talking about the four students who made the "Cindy sandwich"—Arthur, Douglas, Bill, and Rebecca—and their classmates, whom I taught first as an aide then as a teacher of a substantially separate program in their local public high school. The four were very close friends and had been classmates for most of their elementary, middle, and high school years. Their school programs, the product of an ethnically diverse, socioeconomically well-to-do suburb, were individualized until age 22 to meet their specific needs and interests. Their classes consisted of a few elective courses in general education, but mostly functional life skills instruction in separate special education classrooms as well as in-school and community-based supported employment. The program's goal was to prepare them for adult life.

I would prefer to describe these four students in a personal way: Rebecca as a skier and vibrant creative writer who loves reading about the 1960s; Arthur as a scientifically minded young man who likes sports, gadgets, and hieroglyphics; Douglas, who likes language, music, and laughing; and Bill, who likes bowling, being with people, and winning track and field medals. These descriptions honor the students' individuality and touch their essence as people. However, they do little to explain who the students are in this kind of special classroom or why certain tensions arise in teaching them.

A somewhat different way to describe the students would be to say that formal assessments given throughout their schooling typically have labeled these four young adults as individuals with moderate to severe mental retardation. A visitor to their high school would notice easily how different they look and act from other high school students. Rebecca's slanted eyes and elongated Down's Syndrome face mark her as different even before she stutters a word. Douglas's piercing stare and lack of natural movement in his upper torso signal that he too is different. Arthur's tendency to stand far within a stranger's personal space, and Bill's seeming indifference to the world around him, suggest their special needs. The four sometimes understand they have special needs and sometimes do not, rarely investing time in trying to look or act more mainstream. Only Rebecca can reliably cross the street safely on her own. Only Bill would be able to take 5 from 20 in his head, Arthur to ask a stranger for directions without a lot of prompting, or Douglas to memorize the lyrics of rock songs. Arthur drools; Bill emits an odor from incontinence; Douglas speaks to pretty women inappropriately; and Rebecca yells and throws fits when she gets upset. These brief, harsh-sounding characterizations accurately describe part of who these students are, and also help to determine what must be taught. Teaching Arthur to stand at arm's length, and Douglas to swing his arms and move his eyes, will reduce the possibility that they will be characterized negatively by people in the community who have no window into who they really are. Such frank "negative" descriptions, while important from a classroom perspective, would not be tolerated in writing on a report card or an educational plan. Nor would I use this language in casual conversation with strangers.

My various responses to the questions about who I teach reflect how I've been scripted to talk and think about students with disabilities in different contexts. The words I speak in casual conversations or write in reports or describe to other special education teachers or strangers are not just *my* words. In my words live the ventriloquated voices of graduate school, teacher training, public high school administration, fellow teachers, and official educational law, policy, and protocol.

"Monday Talk"

I do not wholly disagree with the three most common descriptions used for students with special needs: that they are concrete, egocentric, and unable to generalize. And yet I think it is dangerous for these statements to drive a teacher's thinking about her students, because there is only some truth to them. A classmate of the four "Cindy sandwich" students was once amazed that anyone could know how many people live in her community. She said they didn't come to her door and count her. She was similarly mystified by the presidential election process. She asked, "How do they know, like, who wins? Do they announce it on a loud speaker or something?" The thought of this actually happening across the whole country made me chuckle to myself. Experience and general knowledge play such a large role in understanding the world, and this student did hard work to synthesize and generalize information from what she knew. After all, using a loudspeaker is a perfectly good way of announcing things to a large number of people at school. The student extrapolated from her context, but not appropriately. Thus, students with special needs do generalize, but have difficulty technically because they don't know when to apply the rules and when not to.

I believed what I had been taught about students with mental retardation. I naturally saw many examples in the classroom that corroborated thinking about them as concrete and egocentric. They certainly had expressive and receptive language difficulties. I thought it was my job to teach them in a way that helped them to remedy their difficulties, and make them more acceptable community members. These beliefs led to the second major assumption about students with special needs, determining how I thought I should teach, that is, with a functional life skills curriculum. This is, in fact, how I taught, and our programs were exceptional programs for these students with disabilities. The students practiced important functional life skills such as taking messages over the phone, ordering a pizza, paying for groceries, telling a doctor their symptoms, settling a disagreement with a friend, asking for an item at the supermarket, and asking for/giving directions. The more tied to real life, the better the curriculum seemed to be.

Monday morning conversations exemplify how I was taught to teach a functional curriculum. For Bill, Rebecca, Douglas, Arthur and their classmates, Monday mornings were a time for structured conversation practice. On Monday mornings, the students shared "what I did on my weekend" stories. A pair of students typically modeled a conversation for the rest of the class. Afterwards, the conversations were examined according to criteria of a "good" conversation: (1) take turns back and forth; (2) look at the person you're talking to; (3) show interest when the other person talks; (4) ask a lot of questions; (5) talk about something in common; (6) expand on the main ideas; (7) match your face emotionally to your words; (8) be specific; and (9) have a beginning and ending.

These "Monday-talk" conversations required complex skills and were very hard for the students. Each student often would take one long detailed turn about him/herself starting with "at 8 o'clock on Friday, I [did this]," sequentially presenting all events until Sunday night, then conclude with, "that's it, your turn," so the other person could tell his/her story. The listeners often acknowledged with "uh huh," "yeah," "OK," or "good," and rarely asked questions or added information. They often did check the clock, look in their laps, signal boredom, stare uncomfortably at the person speaking, or even silently get up to get hot chocolate from across the room right after having directly been asked a question.

Over time, the students gave fewer monologues and used more fluid turn-taking techniques. They were still awkward conversationalists. For instance, Alice and Cody once had what would have been considered by outside observers to be a model conversation following the nine rules. They asked questions like, "What did you do on Saturday?" and, "Where did you eat dinner?" going back and forth and asking each other if they had fun. In short, they got many of the mechanics "right." To an insider, however, the conversation was very strange. Alice and Cody mostly asked questions that sounded like information gathering, but they lived in the same house and had done many of the exact same activities together the past weekend! They knew the answers to their own questions, perhaps just the help they needed to have this conversation so well, or maybe teachers have modeled too well how to form these questions.

In the classroom, I enjoyed finding out what happened on the students' weekend. I thought it was genuinely important and interesting. However, this Monday-talk format made me uncomfortable since the students used only the "form" of language that they had been taught. I realized that the unintentional, primary focus of Monday talk was on *how* the students talked rather than on celebrating *what* they were trying to say. Monday talk was instructional. The students' words were made available for public inspection and were judged on the rules of "good conversation." However, the students were merely ventriloquating through a kind of school talk discourse that was privileged in the classroom. While their talk looked "functional," they weren't communicating in individually meaningful ways. This brings up the question of functional curriculum: "functional for whom?" If we teach with the desire that a student act more like the social norm, are we always sure we are providing instruction that is functional for them to grow as people or are we merely teaching toward what is functional for society? Where is the overlap and how can a teacher be sure individual as well as social functionality is furthered?

Fixing Talk

"She's here!" Arthur emphatically announced one morning, his words leading his only partially seen body and large backpack as he burst through the classroom door with a familiar intensity. As a teacher, I had dozens of options for how to respond to him. And less than a

fraction of time to choose one. I felt sandwiched just as I did on the
street, the different roles of teacher and friend conflicting. To an outside observer, "She's here," may have sounded like a mistaken self-
identification from this young man with developmental delays. "You
mean, 'I'm here!'" I could have said, then waited for him to clarify. I
could have done this in a joking way, teasing him as if he were implying he was a woman. Maybe I should feign misunderstanding and request conversational repair by asking in a matter-of-fact tone, "Who's
here?" to facilitate language development by encouraging a revised,
extended turn. Either of these approaches would have been insincere
since I knew precisely what he was talking about. Arthur had said the
day before that he was excited about seeing his cousin who was arriving from overseas, but he expressed some doubt that she was really
going to visit. Given my knowledge of this "insider information,"
should I rejoice with him and respond, "Great! How's she doing?"?

Arthur no doubt was looking to share information, and also to
celebrate. In that fraction of a second, I was pulled in different directions. Would I create a public or private space in my response? I felt
like celebrating, on the one hand, and being "a teacher" on the other;
perhaps I'd do one and then the other. Special education teachers are
especially good at celebrating students' efforts, but usually before or
after requesting a repair for "faulty" language. A compliment diminished by a slap on the hand. Instinctively, before I could think through
all the options above, I responded with an inquisitive tone and a heightened play of confusion and asked, "Who's here?" I believed that in order
for strangers to understand Arthur's speech, he would have to be a lot
clearer and not make so many assumptions about the listener's ability
to put together the "guess the unclear referent" puzzle; that could be
done only if they knew him well. I thought I was supporting his development of language in the hopes that he would improve his commu-
nicative competence in other settings. I simply was responding as I had
been taught, without the advantage I have now of teacher research
reflection on a moment of discomfort and puzzlement, and those two
words, "She's here."

The response to "fix" language is a functional response. That is,
there is the assumption that Arthur would learn more by clarifying his
language so that he would begin to do so with others. It could be said,
however, that the context was not one of Arthur talking to a stranger.
He knew me well and even may have known that I knew what he was
talking about. He may have managed the situation quite well, taking
into account what could have "worked" in that situation given our
relationship. That is the problem with much functional curriculum in

the classroom setting: We narrowly define the social context within our role of teacher, which alters that context. Practicing talking to a store clerk is best done in the store, but when that cannot be done, it is considered functional curriculum to set up situations that are as representative as possible.

Unfortunately, these situations rely on hypothetical circumstances. To respond genuinely to Arthur in this most "real" situation, I should have admitted that I knew what he was talking about, because I did. Using a functional framework, I "played teacher" to try to make his language work, which it actually would have, but for my response. I was the one who made it nonfunctional for him in that context. How confusing it must be for students when we demand that their language be functional, with the purposes changing all the time! So how could I provide opportunities for students to define their own functions of language? Both how I thought about my students and the resulting teaching style needed to be questioned.

Just as my BTRS colleagues would not take abbreviated explanations of my students at face value, they would not leave this issue of functional curriculum unproblematized. They probed and prodded me and asked for data. What if students with mental retardation were not constrained by an "appropriate" communication skills framework? What do I fear could happen? What would their conversations look like? What individually meaningful functions of language might they have that I was not considering? Could they acquire functional communication skills that typically are recognized as "appropriate" when they are having conversations with each other that are not?

"Friday Talk"

Not surprisingly, when I started backing away from the constraints of my special education assumptions, an entirely new discourse emerged, one quite different from Monday talk. This one happened on Friday mornings when Bill, Arthur, Douglas, and Rebecca went with me to their volunteer positions at a local hospital, "General Hospital." There, in a small isolated room, a world of our own, the students assembled patient information packets. Not coincidentally, we were traveling to this job site when the Cindy sandwich was made.

The "Friday talk" that resulted was foreign territory, with a new native language and set of rules. Almost every communication at General Hospital was transformed through a lens of play. A blowing nose would be commented on with, "here we go again for the second symphony," to be followed inevitably by another nose blowing and a humming of Beethoven's Ninth. Amid this sophisticated play, there were animal noises, pig snorts, dog growls, and so on. When a student needed to go get the sign-in book, it would be announced, "He's going to take a loook and get zee boook.". In short, it was the kind of teaching I'd never want my supervisor to catch me doing. This language play I eventually called "fiddling." One day, noticing that Douglas was not working very hard, I admonished: "Are you working, Douglas?" He answered: "No, I'm fiddling." I reminded him, "You need to be working." He replied, "I need more fiddles." Without losing a beat, now pretty good at joining in, I suggested, "Get them out of the box." He promptly got another stack of the patient packets that he was assembling.

Lengthier "fiddling" conversations that ordinarily would have been bracketed out of the classroom were allowed to continue without my redirection. For example, one day Bill told a story about how "John," one of his mother's college professors, was paralyzed from the neck down due to a racquetball accident. The three guys kept asking one another, "How did he do it?" They decided that to become paralyzed from his neck down he must have hit his head against the wall and twisted his neck. The three guys animatedly debated whether Professor "John" must have been hitting a forehand or backhand at the time he was paralyzed. Bill, Douglas, and Arthur involved their whole bodies, often getting up to replay a shot while describing it. Much to my amazement they continued their conversation, uninterrupted, for nearly 15 minutes. Of even greater bemusement to me, they unanimously decided at the end that "John" must have been hitting a backhand.

The next week at General Hospital, the students carried over this conversation and shared their own scars and debated how the injuries happened. One of them had stitches on his forehead from tripping onto the edge of a table when he was young. He ran his fingers along one edge of the table in front of him, then changed to another, saying, "No, no, it was this edge of the table I hit." What was his reference point? Was the table at home oriented north–south or against the wall? The one at the worksite? Did he remember that it was the short, not the long, side of the table where he hurt himself? Some concrete details were important to them, others to me.

I tried to honor the students' voices and ways of making sense of the world. I let them continue talking without interrupting, even when I was confused about what was being said. I assumed they made sense. This created a very safe space. The students began talking about disabilities, usually concealed in jokes about trading brains for a day, talk about mind readers and psychiatrists, and comparisons of bigger or smaller heads. A student once told me I had a bigger head; the rest agreed and they wanted to trade with me. I had forgotten that for them I always played the role of nondisabled.

One day after sharing elementary school stories for nearly an hour, the students were especially candid about their disabilities. During a quite private and vulnerable moment, I took the following field notes:

> *Arnold:* You know then you have a learning disability?
> *Bill:* No.
> *Arnold:* Me neither. . . . I know now!
> *Bill:* Yeah!
> *Arnold:* Now I know I special needs.

The Friday-talk space allowed for a freeing up of imagination, an opening of boundaries, and a safe space for exploring deep feelings.

"Pepsi on the Rocks"

While these conversations were taking place, Douglas, Arthur, Bill, and Rebecca continued folding and neatly arranging the hospital letters and booklets. To take away the time pressures of trying to understand Friday-talk conversation in action, I began audiotaping it. This Friday-talk transcript I call "Pepsi on the Rocks."

1. *Douglas:* I always used to call him soup, a rock or something. Soup.
2. *Bill:* Scotch on the rocks, if you need ice.
3. *Rebecca:* You're supposed to say Pepsi on the rocks.
4. *Douglas:* How about Roxanne Pepsi on the rocks?
5. *Bill:* How about Diet Pepsi on the rocks?
6. *Rebecca:* How about Cindy on the rocks? How about Cindy on the rocks?
7. *Cindy:* Cindy on the rocks?
8. *Rebecca:* Oh, yes, it would be quite tasty.
9. *Douglas:* Diet Cindy Pepsi on the rocks.
10. *Cindy:* Diet Cindy Pepsi on the rocks?
11. *Rebecca:* Ah yes, that's even better.
12. *Douglas:* Diet Kosher Pepsi Cindy on the rocks.
13. *Bill:* How about Douglas on the rocks?
14. *Douglas:* How about Aerosmith on the rocks? Mr. Roger, Mr. Taylor on the rocks.

This conversation at first seemed just like any other kind of conversation that was happening at the hospital with the students. While I immediately recognized this form of talk, I didn't at all understand its function. The conversation seemed crazy and exclusionary, accessible only to those willing and able to enter the craziness. Especially in the classroom, it would have been easy for me to dismiss this kind of talk as inappropriate and not particularly valuable to developing everyday conversation skills acceptable in adult life. However, by taping this talk, I was able to slow it down and "explode" its meaning. I had a lot of detailed insider knowledge about the students that an outside researcher or observer might not have, and so I can provide the following between-the-lines reading of the transcript:

Out of the blue, as he often does, Douglas said, "I always used to call him soup, a rock or something. Soup." Bill picked up on the word *rock* to take the conversation further. The students were planning for an upcoming prom and often talked about what to drink in the limousine in which they would ride. Thus, Bill in (2) said, "Scotch on the rocks, if you need ice." Rebecca, having strong feelings about alcohol, takes a position against that idea and in (3) admonishes Bill and suggests Pepsi on the rocks as an alternative. This ended the first Douglas, Bill, Rebecca turn-taking sequence. Another similar sequence followed as Douglas joined in the new stream of conversation in (4) by suggesting yet another alternative: "How about Roxanne Pepsi on the rocks?" playing with the nickname Rox for Roxanne, and "rocks." Roxanne was another of their teachers (see Chapter 6) and was helping them with detailed prom arrangements. The students' relationship with Roxanne was so meaningful that even when she was not in the same place with them, she nonetheless influenced and structured their experiences. Bill, a diabetic, then altered his first idea in (5) by adding his personal concerns and suggesting Diet Pepsi. In (6–7) Rebecca tried to engage me in the conversation. I felt obligated to enter after the overture, but without exactly knowing how, so I answered as neutrally as possible and repeated her phrasing in a genuine question. Rebecca acknowledged and welcomed my entry by teasing me in (8): "Oh, yes, it would be quite tasty." Douglas combined two previous thoughts in stating, "Diet Cindy Pepsi on the rocks," in (9), leaving me to wonder whether the Pepsi was diet or he was referring to my being on a diet. I then responded again with a question in (10), and Rebecca accepted that transformation by saying in (11), "Ah yes, that's even better." Douglas responded to this with another synthesis by adding "kosher" to the equation in (12), in an effort to engage Arthur, who kept kosher. Although silent, Arthur was thus given a place in the conversation just as Roxanne was. Then Bill asked in (13): "How about Douglas on the rocks?" Finally, Douglas, who began the conversation with "rock" that Bill first transformed, took the turn back from Bill to effectively end the conversation by once again transforming rock to rock music and asking about the band leaders (14): "How about Aerosmith on the rocks? Mr. Roger, Mr. Taylor on the rocks."

This close examination demonstrates that the students were in fact employing many complexities of communication, playing out sophisticated social interaction strategies. This new reading of Friday talk is most remarkable for its inclusiveness. One by one, rather systematically, the students included participants in their talk. There was no premium put on individual understanding, only on participation to create a collective dialogue and shared meaning. Without being tape-recorded and transcribed, and therefore available for continued reflection, this conversation would seem like just another crazy example of Friday-talk conversation at the hospital worksite.

Friday talk allowed me to see the benefits of letting students talk for themselves. I found that the students were learning new ways of talking and thinking, which was information I needed as a teacher. I was quite uncomfortable with Friday talk, however. While the students learned and indeed improved in terms of the skills they practiced with one another, that progress still did not make inroads toward social acceptance. How could I justify a teaching method that they could not use in the community? Did individually meaningful functions of language use always have to be sacrificed in order to develop social appropriateness? I began to think about how I could structure the classroom so that language use would be both free enough to fulfill individually meaningful functions and structured enough to promote improved language skills. These questions were very important and long-lasting; they transcended my move to another school system with a new group of high school students with special needs.

A TEACHER LEARNING ABOUT WRITING

This second group of special needs high school students that I taught lived in a more socioeconomically depressed working-class community than that of Arthur and his classmates. Like the first group, these were wonderful individuals struggling to make sense of their world, trying to find ways to express honestly who they were to themselves and to others. They wanted desperately to be valued for their core identity and interests, not to be confined by their special education labels. They were interested in what was cool: dating, cars, makeup, music, and clothes.

The students in this second classroom brought with them special needs profiles that were somewhat different from those of Arthur, Rebecca, Bill, and Douglas. They typically scored in the borderline range on IQ tests, between low average and mildly mentally retarded. They were "less retarded" on paper. I mention these scores and labels only because in this school system, they predicted rather well what program the students would participate in. Their IQ scores also suggested the students' unique position: one foot in the mainstream world and the other in the special education world, another "sandwiched" position. They resented their program placement, knew they had disabilities, and wanted to deny and hide them. Like Arthur and his classmates, these students had the option to stay in school until they were 22 years of age, but, unlike them, most did not. While Arthur and his classmates shared a deep friendship, these students were uncomfortable hanging out with one another, as if it reminded them of a part of themselves that they tried hard to disown. They valued outside friendships more. Physically, these students blended with the other high school students. They walked the halls during passing time and returned after the bell had rung so the other students did not see which classroom they entered. The students who challenged themselves in this "borderline" program sometimes felt that their choice was to "progress" to taking classes where they felt like the dumbest mainstream kid or to stay in my program as the smartest special needs kid; neither choice was appealing. Some, wanting neither of these, underachieved their potential as if to remain in the safety of my program. The several who achieved the opportunity to leave felt proud and expressed their superiority to the others. At the same time, they intensely resisted, managing to push back the moving out timeline for a marking quarter or two.

The students' borderline position required teaching strategies that were somewhat different from those required in the more classic special needs classroom of Rebecca, Arthur, Douglas, and Bill, where the focus was mostly on *functional life skills* training. But the same position also set them apart from the mainstream, where students focus mostly on *academics*. The students spent most of the day in my classroom in a program that served students with language-based disabilities through a hybrid of these two worlds—*functional academics*.

Just as this second group of students were sandwiched between two worlds, so was I. Additional demands were placed on me in this classroom where I was pressured to teach two kinds of functional curricula.

Specifically, I was expected to focus on remediating their language-based disabilities by teaching academic writing skills, including how to write outlines, reports, summaries, and essays, and how to answer test questions—anything that would help them survive in the next-higher-level academic program if they could earn a ticket out of my class. In contrast, teaching a functional life skills writing curriculum demanded some of the following: practice in writing notes to a friend, making a shopping list, filling out job applications, taking phone messages, writing thank-you letters, ordering from catalogues, and so on. I was expected to teach both sets of skills through "functional academics."

This second group of students had higher cognitive skills than the earlier group, although the descriptions in their academic records were strikingly similar; they were described as concrete and egocentric thinkers who were highly dependent on personal experience to make sense of language tasks. In many ways, this description was true, as noted in the following example where *concrete* and *general* nouns evoked the sidewalk pavement and military officers leading their troops.

Field Notes—English class

I was trying to help the students learn about the different kinds of nouns, those that referred to actual things like *house* and those that were more abstract like *happiness*. This kind of knowledge is on the state test. The students seemed bored. They said this was too easy. I decided to introduce the terms *concrete* and *general*. I explained that even the regular ed kids had trouble with these terms. Hanna said (referring to *general*) That's silly, if you said [that] to one of them (pointing out in the hall), they'd say there's no wars in here. This is school." Leah then followed with, "yeah, and they'd say *concrete*'s on the sidewalk, that's what you walk on." Both girls showed no understanding of the different meanings of these words or the context in which I was using them.

In another example, for 2 weeks in science class we studied, took notes on, wrote about, and talked about ideas in the book *50 Ways to Save the Earth*. One day, the class was reviewing why certain things were harmful to the environment. On almost every topic, I heard answers that, although good, really weren't answering the question I had intended to ask. After several questions in a row with the form, "Why is [styrofoam] bad for the environment?" I asked, "Why are flea collars bad?" only implying "for the environment." Some of them remembered that there are a lot of chemicals that eventually get into our streams after hundreds of thousands of flea collars are thrown into landfills every year. One student answered, "If you pull on the flea collar too much it hurts the dog." True. She answered my question in the strictest sense. Similarly, when asked, "Why is it not a good idea to let balloons go?" (they eventually end up in the ocean and kill fish and other ocean life), a student answered, "I want to keep them. They're fun." It was a good reason, and he gave evidence for his thinking. In both these cases, the students weren't thinking of the context of my question, the review class, or the environment, but rather outlined reasonable circumstances based on their concrete experiences.

I point out the above examples not to highlight what the students cannot do, but rather to show how complicated language is for them. In many cases, I was asking the wrong questions, or the students were interpreting them in more interesting ways than the strict academic way of understanding and demonstrating knowledge that I was looking for.

Traditional academic writing that is neat and well organized with correct spelling, punctuation, and grammar was also very challenging for these students. They struggled with the concept of a topic sentence and supporting argument. I assigned a choice of persuasive essays once, and a student wrote the following topic sentence: "The school's smoking policy is good/bad," with the bad circled. He continued by explaining that it is bad "because if you are with a person that is smoking you can get in trouble." We practiced and practiced, and it was often frustrating for them. While mastery of these skills may lead to better scores on state tests and better chances of acceptance to trade programs, the skills themselves are highly questionable as essential to performing well in future jobs. At the same time, my "borderline" group of students were insulted when given functional life skills tasks. They *wanted* to be mainstream and to do traditional school kinds of writing and study something "hard" like the rest of the high school—which was partly my motivation to teach them concrete and general nouns.

However, more purely functional, less academic writing proved to be equally challenging. Once when Tara actually applied for a real job, she exclaimed while filling out the application: "What's my last name?! Yeah, like I don't know my last name!" Did she think that this was a test from her potential employer? What function did she imagine writing her name had? It was hard to teach her all the different possible application formats and questions. Visually, she got confused about where to write down information. She did not have a good idea of how personal she should get.

The question was always present: With graduation nearing for some of the students, should I teach functional writing tasks or school writing tasks? Each of these would take years for them to master, if they ever did. My questions about writing were similar to my tensions with oral language teaching. I again began to ask "functional for whom?" Should I target language that was appropriate for my supervisor, for what I thought I should teach, or for the student at home, at work, or in school? I also wondered whether the "concrete" and "contextually based" nature of the functional academic curriculum privileged the teaching of skills that were "useful" at the expense of what was "meaningful" to the students.

The academic writing tasks and functional academic writing that I was doing with this group felt a lot like "Monday talk": essential, but not complete. I was willing to teach academic literacies, but not to the exclusion of all else. I tried to find a balance that both the students and I were comfortable with, and kept looking for other ways to help them feel confident about their language use. I wondered what the corollary to "Friday talk" would look like for this group. Maybe I could teach writing in a way that simply allowed students to express themselves for personally defined intentions. What would their writing look like? I decided to start asking the students to write a lot, without the typical teaching restrictions I had been taught regarding editing and notions of "proper" written language.

Free Writing

All I knew was that I wanted the students to love language and writing. They looked for doors out of my classroom, and I sought to help them see the unique worthiness inside of themselves as a ticket to acceptance. Are "loving writing" and "exploring their inner selves" functional? What use of this could they possibly make in their post-school lives? We started doing "word game Friday" during which we played language puzzles, and we wrote a lot of collaborative stories in small groups, or simultaneously wrote 10 stories, by passing the paper and adding to the previous person's sentence in ways that made sense to the cohesion of the story (this was very hard!). In addition, I decided that if nothing else, they would write a lot every day in their English journals. I thought that journal writing would be a good beginning to developing their own individual writing voice.

I knew writing was going to be very hard for them. Peter Elbow, in *Writing Without Teachers* (1973), discusses this difficulty as he compares the demands of speaking and writing.

> Think of the difference between speaking and writing. Writing has the advantage of permitting more editing. But that's its downfall too. Almost everybody interposes a massive and complicated series of editing between the time words start to be born into consciousness and when they finally come off the end of the pencil or typewriter onto the page. This is partly because schooling makes us obsessed with the "mistakes" we make in writing. Many people are constantly thinking about spelling and grammar as they try to write. (pp. 4–5)

The borderline position of my students made them especially self-conscious about their writing. In the beginning, they constantly asked me to spell words for them; 15 out of 15 words, times 10 students. When they couldn't write what they wanted to say, they quit in frustration. Some of them cried. They feared making mistakes and knew from experience in school that most of what they wrote would be mistakes. They hoped that if they mutinied I would not ask them to write anymore. I gave them a clear message that the focus on writing was not going to disappear.

However, I knew that in order to keep them engaged, I would have to relieve them of some of the writing pressures that Elbow referred to. I took away all of the language constraints I could think of. For the most part, I did not grade spelling and punctuation, handwriting, grammar, or what they wrote about. I began to assign free-topic writing. This certainly would be difficult to explain to my supervisor, who thought I was routinely doing job applications and letters. It also would be difficult if I needed to justify why I wasn't filling their notebooks with red ink to point out their errors. Rather, I had them "just write." Not essays, not reports. They wrote and wrote, sentences and paragraphs in their writing journals.

I thought that free topics, where they were required to generate ideas from ground zero, would be a struggle for them. Even choosing a starting point, given a topic, was quite challenging, despite a lot of discussion beforehand. However, it quickly turned out that it was not nearly as difficult for them to enjoy free writing as I had thought. When I later asked them what kind of writing they liked best, they unanimously responded with a roar of "free topic." I stopped giving directed writing assignments, yet still wondered: Why are free topics working so well for them? I asked them.

The students explained to me why they liked free topics: "Because you can write about like how you feel, and what's happening to your life," one student said. Another thought: "When you write you can express your feelings if something is bothering you, you can get it all out and then you can feel better without saying it." New students were always told, "Ms. Beseler lets you write about girlfriends or anything!"

Previously they had had such topics bracketed from their writing. Craig eloquently explained to the class why writing was so powerful to him.

> It relaxes me, I can get it out. I can put it on paper and no one will talk back to me. No one try to convince me or anything. And you just write it and put it aside and don't look at it . . . or if you write a three-page report and someone looks at it and says oh this is wrong, this is wrong, this could use a little more work, and it's like, wait a minute, I just wanted to write it down!

Free topics took the constant need for editing out of the assignment. Craig continued:

> You don't get interrupted when you're trying to say something. And you don't get like feedback with it like aw, you should do this, do this, you should be doing that.

While Craig was talking, several other students were brainstorming about writing "graffiti-style" on a large poster board. I began to read their comments out-loud, and then the following exchange took place:

Teacher: I also see the word *feelings* a lot in here.
Craig: Your feelings come out like differently. If you're trying to talk to someone, you don't say as much like cause you want to keep it in, you want to keep it to yourself. Or you want to express it. But it's like, you want to express it but you're afraid of what's gonna happen after you say it. So if you put it on a piece of paper, you can say it.
Shelley: If you say it to the person you can't explain it right, but then more words—
Craig: Like if I like Shelley and she asks me why, I'll say I don't know, like wait a minute—
Shelley: But on a piece of paper, then I know.
Craig: I can't explain it why. It's weird.
Teacher: How do you think writing and speaking are different, or how are they the same?
Craig: They're the same because you use the same words, but if you write you don't get like feedback back, you don't get someone like yell, like mad at you or whatever.

Peter Elbow (1973) wrote that free-writing helps you by providing "no feedback at all" (p. 4). Craig knew that so well!

Although the students were less anxious about their writing, were putting pen to paper more than ever before, and were even enjoying the writing process, I was becoming increasingly uncomfortable. They were writing about the same topics over and over and over again. Many of their stories, frankly, were boring to read. They simply reported events that happened to them. It reminded me of the early Monday morning conversations where each person methodically described what happened, then turned it over to the next speaker without deliberate connection with an audience. Why or how they were using the writing and what they were learning from it were still not clear to me. I was spending a lot of time letting the students "write," but I found that I wasn't even sure if it was "teaching." My "functional for whom" question was far from answered and I wasn't doing the purely "functional" curriculum that I had been taught I should be doing.

Daniel's Writing

I began to take a closer look at the students' writing to try to understand how free-writing was serving or not serving their learning needs. The writing of Daniel, a senior, especially concerned me. Daniel loved being a teenager, having a car, and hanging out with friends. But all he seemed to write about was cars: 90% of his free-topic writing mentioned cars. Even if I assigned a topic, he found a way to include cars. His writing seemed inflexible, egocentric, concrete, and repetitive. Below is Daniel's first piece of free-topic journal writing.

The new Chevrolet
Impala/SS/1996

The Impala SS has leather intereor
The Impals SS has a lotts of
option for the new year. I got
a new car it is A tran Am. I when
to the beach and I mat New friends.
I when to New Hamsher

Daniel's first writing piece resembled straightforward reporting. As a reader, I was bored. Daniel seemed to be talking about three different topics, and I didn't know how they connected because he didn't yet know how to make those connections explicit in his writing. While the depth of his interest in cars resulted in detail the rest of the class struggled with, his writing was simply an inward-focused description.

Daniel produced dozens and dozens of similar pieces of writing. Nearly 3 months later, Daniel wrote about this first piece of writing on a small index card to highlight it as one of his three most important pieces of writing during first quarter.

The Impala SS

I put a lot of work in The Story
I like talkin a But cars.
I rely talk a lot But cars. I
Love cars. I met a lot of New
friends.

I think that by choosing his first piece of writing, Daniel was signaling how significant beginning the act of writing was to him, although he still couldn't say why, beyond mentioning how much work he put into it and how much he liked the subject matter. I learned from this writing what the connection was among the three topics: Cars take him to places and people that are important. Cars symbolize freedom and connect him with what is meaningful. In Daniel's very next piece of writing, he again wrote about cars and friends. He wrote about driving to the beach, taking friends for a ride, and having people admire his car. He positioned himself as a writer more *in* the car and ended with a quite poetic, "My car look like a bird with the wing." That was his first poetry.

A month after beginning to write, Daniel went deeper into the personal perspective, explaining how deeply cars really got under his skin.

If there one thing I know
for sure it's this car's.
I loved car's when I was a bady.
My kid's a going to lean a
lot adout cars. Me and my friend
know a lots about
cars. When I would clean my
car. He would clean car. My car
come out the best.

Here, he used writing and cars to understand his passion and how he positioned himself in life. At the same time, the writing was somehow less egocentric. Writing about cars was the vehicle for him to make sense of the world around him, including competition and relationships. He included a friend in this piece of writing in a new way. He was not just reporting but rather constructing a narrative.

In October, a month later, Daniel wrote the following:

A Day at work
vala parking

I drove a Catic. You can
have fun Driving other people cars.
You can Drive like a nut. You
Donot pay tekets. there is no
packing in Boston. Ther are
to many police. There are to many
police a round. Thay will not
let my Drive standerd. I want to
Drive A 6 speed Corvett. Car are
the Best.

This was actually an imaginary piece, which moved further away from the concrete. I am quite sure Daniel never did valet parking. Here was a great dream—to think about a Cadillac so carefree, tempered by a bit of reality that there are rules he still would have to follow. He did his first editing when he rephrased "there are too many police" to "there are too many police around."

Although most of Daniel's writing started off with the formula, "I went to a car show, I saw a [blank]," once in very long while he produced other kinds of writing. In these instances, Daniel wrote about important teenage topics like going egging on Halloween or friends dying. In November, Daniel wrote one of his rare noncar pieces.

The first Day of snowed

We are going to have a
Bad winter. We are
going to By a snow Blower.
Snow is very fun to play with
Snow spelles truble. I Donot
relly like snow. It nice to lock
at. It is nice look at the iceicacles
If you see snow for
a will you will get sek
of it. You can look at

so much. But were would the
water go. I wish it snowed
all year round. I would Be so nice.

This was as close to a compare and contrast academic writing piece as I had seen Daniel write. He thought about snow being fun on the one hand, and trouble on the other, including reasons why. He also used writing for the first time to wonder ("Where would the water go?") and wish ("I wish it snowed all year round").

In December, Daniel wrote about cars with so much enthusiasm and passion that as a reader I thought I almost liked cars. Unlike his first writing, I wasn't in the least bored.

I went on a car show. we
saw a Ferra it was Red on Black.
It had 17teen inch rimes. I wish I
had that car. that car will
turn every wone will turn ther
head. I had a V12 engen. It
has so meny wiches. You would
go crazzy. The top speed
is /220 Mph. After the show I went to
my girlfriend house. I went to
see her parends. She Live faraway
She live in Salem Ma.

The context was set, the detail was good, and the emotion in this piece was extraordinary. He took on the audience's perspective, as if trying to excite readers by giving them ideas about how they would feel in his place. His use of "you" and "their" emerged as a particularly interesting shifting of voice.

In January, violence was a topic that was on the students' minds a lot due to several incidents at the school, one of which resulted in the death of a student whom my students knew, at least by sight. After a very long discussion one day, I assigned "violence" as the topic that they were to write about in class. This was a rare departure I would make in their "journal time." Daniel wrote:

Car Show fight

I went to a inDoor car
show. I saw a red caloway

> I saw someone person throw a punch
> My friend got punche in his
> sholder. I got punched after. We
> went to go fine the kid it was
> my friend foster Bother. He
> Does not live with him now. We
> called him outside. We punched
> Him in his shoulder. We tould him
> if he was got to throw punches
> we would hit him twis as
> hard. We have not herd
> for him latelet.

This story has such a wonderful sense of humor. It contains plot, drama, description, and resolution. Daniel chose not to deal directly with his friend's death, but did so indirectly by commenting on his relationship with violence.

Some days the writing task was to re-read and edit current or past writing. In the above piece, Daniel did a lot of editing, including crossing out, re-spelling, deleting, and adding. By February, Daniel had really taken a liking to the process of editing. He wrote on one of his "best of the quarter" index cards:

> This store was the Best
> Because This was the Best.
> I started to Edit my store
> Edit can Be so fun.

Here is the story he was talking about:

The Best Class

> A Day the teache
> Ascined Set.
>
> I was seting in the far Back.
> I was write bout Ascined sets
> we had a free topic in class.
> I had a excellent topic going. The class
> was a mass. people were
> Talk out of control and out of hand. I start
> out have a ruff and the worst day.

The Day got Better. My last period. I had
a nice time. My other class
were all right. When you got to High
School thay give you a had time
on avything. I thout MonDay are
Bad. A Thursday can Be wers
ThursDay can be very
Bad. I mean Bad!!!

This story demonstrated an unusual amount of reflectiveness, providing a remarkable contrast to his first rather egocentric writings.

By the end of the year, Daniel's last one in high school, the progress he had made in his writing was very subtle: He took others' points of view, elaborated his thoughts, edited for his audience, wondered, dreamed, and wrote plot and resolution in his small one-paragraph stories. Worth more than any of the small improvements from the beginning of the year, however, was that Daniel felt better about his ability to write, and so he risked himself to write more in all of his classes. He and his classmates had fun re-reading their stories to choose their favorite writing every quarter. They often exclaimed, "Oh, this was a good one!" and were amazed at how much they had improved as writers over time. They felt proud of themselves and often couldn't wait for me to read something they had written. The students immersed themselves in their words and discovered they were valuable and worth writing and reading about.

However, Daniel had really made only a very small amount of academic progress with his writing overall: It still needed considerable improvement and definitely was not adequate to write essays for a state test, or perhaps even to support his wish to go to community college or work as an auto mechanic. I wondered about my teaching choice to help the students feel better about their abilities versus encouraging some improvement in school types of writing, but with less self-esteem. In the classroom, though, the choice really was clear: Writing may have been important for their success, but a sense of self-worth was very, very important to even grander definitions of success.

Daniel and his classmates usually felt so excruciatingly "edited" in every aspect of their lives, as if they had to become someone else to succeed, that it prevented them from reaching their potential. These students previously had been demoralized by public discussion of their writing and by having to write in ways that bracketed out what was meaningful to them. They wanted meaningful ways to communicate, and communication was especially complex for them given their disabilities. Again, Peter Elbow (1973) comments: "Meaning in ordinary language is in the middle. It is pushed and pulled simultaneously by forces that try to make it fluid and dreamlike but also fixed like mathematics." He describes the language of mathematics where things mean only what publicly acknowledged rules allow them to mean. Dreaming, on the other hand, he says, has no audience and "is all speaking and no listening: dreams are for the sake of dreaming, not for the sake of interpreting" (p. 153). This is the push and pull of my special needs students. They were enthusiastic about free-writing, when they essentially could create their own writing curriculum and put it to use in personally defined ways. That is, they could make it functional for themselves. When they began choosing to edit their own writing for their own purposes, they were rewriting who they were and their dreams for who they could become, and that seemed worthwhile. If I was going to ask them to dream of futures where society would accept them as more valued, I had to create talking and writing spaces for them to dream themselves into their potential. That is functional.

CONCLUSION

This story began with the "Cindy sandwich" metaphor describing tensions I felt due to the multiple interpretations and expectations of the role of "teacher." I stated that the ways I had been taught to talk about, think about, and teach learners with special needs were sometimes in conflict with how I ordinarily would want to interact with them as human beings. I also suggested that learners with special needs have been taught to speak and write through school or societal norms, often in conflict with how they naturally reveal themselves to the world; they too feel sandwiched, and this has been their story too. I conveyed my discomfort with a functional curriculum typically prescribed for students with special needs, and posed the question, "Functional for whom?"

Also threaded throughout this story was that of how a teacher research framework helped me to redefine the boundaries of teaching and learning in my classrooms. It was with my colleagues' probing questions and genuine interest in what was best for students, and with the hindsight of field notes and a tape recorder, that I was able to explore the tension I had about my teaching, raise questions about functional curriculum, and confidently take informed risks to teach kids with special needs in new ways that honored them. In retrospect, I realize how easy it was for me as a teacher to constantly reword, edit, question, and herd students' talk and writing so that it stayed within the confines of appropriateness. When I dismantled this imposed need, the students were liberated from the constant editing of their speaking and writing, and I was free to see how much sense they actually were making as I paid attention to what the students intended to say (that is, what was individually functional for them) rather than on how they said it.

I believe my story is more than simply a story about my personal growth as a teacher or relevant only to my group of students. The teacher research framework, accessible to all teachers, values a teacher's ability to see the classroom from within. With acknowledgment of our expertise and careful consideration of our craft over a period of time within our own classroom environments, we can research what does and does not work, and dismantle imposed structures when necessary. That is not to say that structures such as functional curriculum must be disregarded. On the contrary, my examination of functional curriculum allowed me to see more clearly its benefits as well as drawbacks for my particular students.

Similarly, I would not be able to suggest with certainty that either Monday talk, Friday talk, or free-writing, as described in this story, would be beneficial for other particular special needs groups. Yet, I do believe that the questions that drove me to the innovations I tried are ones other teachers could benefit from asking too. For instance, the descriptions of students as concrete, egocentric, and unable to generalize are cognitive styles, if you will, that have real implications in the classroom and do demand consideration in teaching choices. I don't deny that there is some truth to them. However, I feel very uncomfortable with our shorthand descriptions that threaten to abbreviate the students themselves, by a full characterization of them. It is dangerous for these statements to drive a teacher's thinking about her students because with that lens we fail to recognize the students' use of complex skills.

Labeling students as concrete, egocentric, and unable to generalize emphasizes deficits and leads to programs to remedy deficits—the students would need to learn skills that are important for them to get along in current and future environments of work, home, school, and community. Even if implemented by building on the students' strengths (necessarily as they match those needed in the community), this approach is important but exclusionary. There are many other kinds of learning that need to take place, based on students' strengths (ways of talking or writing that we may not immediately understand or value highly), that often do not get space in traditional special education curricula.

A student once asked me, after inquiring about my school experience: "Why are you teaching here if you weren't in special needs classes?" She asked, "Why would I want to?" as if she thought no one would be there who didn't have to be, as if she thought I were a special needs teacher and a teacher with special needs! No amount of more correct spelling, talking, or writing will make a special needs student feel completely valuable in school, worthy of the time of nonspecial education people, because they always know how much more they have to learn to be like "the other students." Self-esteem, knowing one's value and worth, is something best taught not from outside skills, but rather from the inside of the student. We must open at least some amount of space in our special education classrooms for this kind of learning to take place, no matter how much it may be at odds with our traditional teaching beliefs. Maybe that space will not raise test scores immediately, but with good teacher research and careful risk taking, the students will feel valued and create their own space in the world.

CHAPTER 5

In Search of an Honest Response

JIM SWAIM

I am a third-grade teacher who has been teaching the writing process for a very long time. In that time, almost 20 years, I found myself becoming increasingly confused by the writing behavior of children in my classroom. In an effort to better understand what was happening in writing workshop, I turned to teacher research and in 1991 began my affiliation, which continues today, with the BTRS. Writing workshop occurs every morning for an hour. After a short, teacher-directed minilesson, the children write silently for 10 minutes. For the next 20 minutes they have the choice of continuing to write, working on drafts, publishing, or having a conference with a teacher or peer. In a peer conference, the author chooses a partner, then reads her/his story out-loud and decides, with the partner's input, what type of changes could be made. The last 10 minutes of the workshop is a class sharing session where an author shares his/her writing piece with the entire class.

Best described by one class member as "a shop with stories," writing workshop in my class shows authors at various stages in the writing process: wrestling with ideas, composing a draft, revising, and preparing to publish. This particular shop does not specialize in one type of product, but, instead, offers personal narratives, poems, sports stories, fantasies, adventures, mysteries, plays, and anything else that fulfills the rule, "write what you know and care about." Throughout the year authors work at their own pace and make their own decisions on whether a completed, revised draft is worthy of publication. One expectation is that authors have at least three conferences with a peer on a particular piece of writing. The hope is that by experiencing the roles of both writer and audience, the authors' decision to publish or not would be an informed one.

This chapter describes my efforts to better understand what transpires when children share their writing together. Embedded in this

An earlier version of this chapter first appeared as "In Search of an Honest Response" by Jim Swaim in *Language Arts*, vol. 75, no. 2, pp. 118–125. Copyright © 1999 by the National Council of Teachers of English. Reprinted by permission.

account is a description of how theory and practice changed for me and how my role as teacher researcher allowed this to happen.

Motivated by my confusion over the lack of substantive revision by writers after a conference, I first focus on the issue of peer response in conferences and class sharing sessions. Then I depict the evolution of a fictional story entitled "The Man Who Was Late for Dinner" written by a third grader named Pamela. This story occurred during a year when I made substantial changes to the way I taught writing. It represents for me the writing culture that emerged in my classroom that year and whose members, as they interacted, began to lead me toward answers to two questions that had plagued me for a long time: How can children connect through their writing? and what constitutes an honest response to this writing?

PEER RESPONSE

I began my research by recording children as they met to discuss works in progress or final drafts. We set up a designated recording area in the classroom reading loft where children were invited to tape-record conferences. In one recorded interaction, Lee and Susan discuss Lee's story, "The House on the Hill in the Night." The story is about a boy who is eaten by a monster and then reunited with his parents who had been eaten by the same monster 3 years before. The story describes how the boy slides down the monster's throat into his stomach and finds his parents playing checkers in the belly of the monster. The boy tries several times to escape and eventually does. Lee and Susan conclude their conference with a significant discussion about detail.

> *Lee:* I don't know. I just have this feeling that I did not put enough detail into it. Do you think I put enough detail or maybe too much?
>
> *Susan:* I think it was pretty good. I mean if you want to change it you can.
>
> *Lee:* Yeah, I did work really hard but I have a feeling I either put too little or too much detail.
>
> *Susan:* Well, I think in some parts there was too much detail and in some parts there was too little like when you said about the checker and how did they get the checkers?
>
> *Lee:* I think I'm going to add and put in a page there and stuff. Do you think I should tape all my pages together so that it won't be hard?

Susan: No.
Lee: Do you like my story?
Susan: Yeah.

While the girls seemed earnest and clearly on task during this conference, they did not focus on points of confusion, challenge one another for explanations or elaboration, or even address one another by name. Words and phrases that I had taught during mini-lessons on revision permeated the conference. This led me to an unsettling hypothesis: Perhaps my attempt to predetermine and define the terms that Susan and Lee used in their conference prevented them from actually using or even inventing their own language for revising their writing.

Both girls were versed in the language of revision, but not in the actual knowledge of how to revise. Bloome (1987) refers to this as "procedural display." It occurs when both teacher and student are most concerned with displaying a set of procedures or routines in a lesson. Although I was not present during the conference, my voice and expectations clearly were. Lee's and Susan's sole goal in this conference was to converse using the terms I had taught them in the mini-lessons. The conference itself had a hollow, unnatural quality to it as though the girls were following a script and could deliver their lines but didn't understand the meaning of what they were saying. The central issue of how to revise Lee's story was lost amid the display of terms. In the end, revision was reduced to adding one small detail about how the checkers came to be in the belly of the monster. By stressing the need to use these terms in scripted conversations, I prevented children from responding on their own terms with their own language to the real content of stories.

If procedural display was hindering natural conversation and an honest response to writing during peer conferences, then was the same thing happening in the larger context of class sharing sessions? Had my role as a teacher of the language of revision so conditioned me that I, like the children, was most concerned with the display of routine and procedure? I decided to focus on class sharing as I had on peer conferences by listening carefully and slowly to what children said to each other.

CLASS SHARING

One day in February, Diane and Lee sat in the author's chair and shared the first draft of a picture book entitled "The Sun and the Little Girl." They prefaced their reading by noting that Diane had written the story specifically for kindergartners and that she had recruited Lee as her illustrator.

The story recounts the adventures of a little girl named Judy who has just moved into a new house. On the first day she unsuccessfully scours the neighborhood for new friends. On the second day, lonely and forlorn, she finally looks up in the sky and sees the sun smiling down on her. The sun, whose name is Jimmy, can communicate with Judy, but cannot move from his position in the sky. Judy suggests that they play a game together. Mindful that the sun cannot leave his position, they finally decide that the only game they are physically able to play together is Hide-and-Go-Seek. The sun is "it" first and finds Judy hiding under a tree. Judy goes next and discovers the sun hiding behind a cloud. The story ends when three of Judy's friends arrive. Judy tells her friends, "Let's go play. I have a new friend. His name is Jimmy." "Where is your friend?" asks one of the friends. "Up there," replies Judy.

Mark begins the response part of the share with a question about the number of words on each page of the story, "Aren't there too little words on each page? Are there five on each page?" "It's a rough draft," says Lee, "and we want to draw pictures underneath it because we are doing it for kindergartners." Next David asks how the sun, given its position in the sky, is able to see Judy.

> *David:* How could the sun see down on the earth and like the sun is as high as anything?
> *Lee:* It's fantasy, David.
> *Danny:* It's only for kindergartners.
> *Stuart:* David, David, if you see, your sight never ends. You will see forever unless something blocks it.
> *Susan:* The higher you are, the more you can see.
> *Stuart:* Let's say you are here, and there's a hill down like that and you're over here. You can't see. Your sight never ends. It goes on forever.
> *Susan:* But the higher you are the more you can see because you can see over things.
> *Diane:* Well, you guys, it's not all the way up in the sky. It's low down.

Perhaps if the authors had read this story to a kindergarten class as originally intended, the audience might have responded differently to the playful personification and issues of friendship in the story. That kind of authentic, personalized response would have affirmed the authors' intentions and focused on content, rather than on scientific accuracy. Instead, in a vivid example of talk being shaped by its own momentum, a vocal minority, either consciously or unconsciously, shunned the stated intentions of the authors and chose instead to engage in science talk. Their response focused on what the text ought to have been rather than what it really was. Because the class did not respond to the real intentions of the story, the authors came away from this interaction feeling diminished and excluded.

By analyzing these two interactions, I gained insight into the ways that children in my class responded to one another's writing. In both cases children had a difficult time reacting to the content and intentions of the writing. In the case of the peer conference, the need for procedural displays made attending to the text impossible. Instead of examining real issues like loss of parents or the experience of being trapped, both girls felt compelled to talk like the teacher. In class sharing, children examined the scientific basis for Diane's story instead of responding reflectively to a fantasy written for kindergartners. The response of the audience in both cases did little to motivate the writer to write more. Lee and Susan felt successful and complacent because they had performed well, not because they had revised Lee's story. Diane and Lee felt misinterpreted and defensive and only wanted to read their story to a more receptive audience.

That year I was forced to look more closely at my role in creating a writing culture that rarely responded to content, and to seek an answer to what I meant by "honest response and natural connection through writing." Ironically, the answer emerged in a book written primarily for children.

HONEST RESPONSE AND NATURAL CONNECTION

In *The Bat-Poet*, Randall Jarrell (1964) tackles the issues of connection and response for early writers. It is the story of a bat who, unable to sleep during the day, begins writing poetry about the mysterious new world of daylight. He models his poems after the songs of the mockingbird whom he greatly admires. Finally he gets up enough courage to share with the mockingbird his first poem, which is about his own night world and the predatory owl. The mockingbird responds, "Why, I like it. Technically, it's quite accomplished. The way you change the rhyme-scheme's particularly effective." The mockingbird goes on to applaud "the next-to-last line's iambic pentameter and the last line's iambic trimeter" (p. 14). The bat returns home, thinking about the mockingbird's response.

Partly he felt very good—the mockingbird had liked his poem—and partly he felt just terrible. He thought, "Why, I must just as well have said it to the bats. What do I care about how many feet it has? The owl nearly kills me, and he says he likes the rhyme-scheme. . . . The trouble isn't making the poems, the trouble is finding somebody that will listen to them." (pp. 14–15)

The bat seeks another audience, this time with the chipmunk. The chipmunk's response is decidedly different. He finds the poem disturbing. "It's terrible, just terrible! Is there really something like that at night? I'm going to bed earlier. Sometimes when there're lots of nuts I stay out till it's pretty dark, believe me, I'm never going to again" (p. 17). Upon a second reading, the chipmunk says, "It makes me shiver. Why do I like it if it makes me shiver?" (p. 22). The poet is so pleased with this authentic response that he offers to write a poem for the chipmunk.

My response to this wonderfully allegorical tale was similar to the chipmunk's. It made me shiver. The world created by Jarrell might just as well have been my classroom, with the response of the mockingbird the norm, rather than the exception. It seemed that the bat's dilemma of finding someone to "listen" to his poems was similar to Diane's and Lee's. Like the mockingbird, my class had fixated on the form of the story, and Diane had come away from the interaction discouraged and defensive and, like the bat, feeling "just terrible."

Most teachers of the writing process will acknowledge the importance of social interaction in the language-learning process. Teachers and peers need to talk to one another about writing and their reaction to that writing. Yet, there are some kinds of talk or modes of response that are more helpful than others to the writer. *The Bat-Poet* highlighted two types of response that affected the bat quite differently. The mockingbird's response gives the appearance of being sensitive, polite, and instructive. Such a response often is modeled by the teacher so that it is part of the explicit curriculum. It is designed to help beginning writers see what works in their writing. Appearances in the classroom, however, are sometimes deceiving, and when we listen carefully to the voices of writers in writing workshop, or get inside their heads as Jarrell allows us to do with the bat, we find that the effect of the response is quite the opposite of its initial aim. The bat has no use for the mockingbird's comments about the metric structure in his poem because that was not his intention in the first place. Through the poem, he wanted to show the pure terror of his nearly fatal experience with the dreaded owl. When the response does not acknowledge the writer's intentions, it can have a very discouraging effect on the writer and his/her desire to write more.

The second mode of response embodies what I would call the honest response. It is honest because the response honors the intentions of the writer and the reasons for writing. When the chipmunk heard the bat's poem a second time, he responded in a profoundly human way: "It makes me shiver. Why do I like it if it makes me shiver?" Perplexed as he was, the chipmunk had shown the bat the affective power of his writing. It was the response of the chipmunk, not the mockingbird, that convinced the bat to keep writing poetry. The chipmunk had shown the bat that his writing was meaningful, real, and socially embedded in the culture of the woods. No wonder the bat offered to write his next poem about and for the chipmunk. It was a natural connection.

CHANGES IN PRACTICE

My research had shown me that I too had adopted the voice of the mockingbird when I responded to children's fiction. The transcripts of peer conferences and class sharing indicated that Diane, Susan, and the rest of the class had embraced this voice also. For next year's class I was determined to change my practice and reconstruct writing workshop so that the honest response and natural connection could happen more frequently.

In mini-lessons I limited my use of words associated with revision (pruning, expanding, revising, editing, etc.). I was less dogmatic about the purposes of a conference. Children no longer had to meet in pairs. They were encouraged to meet in larger groups and to use the time to read their stories out-loud and react to them. The job of the author no longer was to come away from the conference with something to change in the draft. Instead they were asked only to acknowledge and remember the audience's reaction. Conversely, the job of the audience was to find something in the draft that evoked an emotional response in them and to articulate this reaction as best they could to the author—a tall order for third graders!

The notion of collaboration was introduced early in the year. As defined in mini-lessons, collaboration meant two things. First, two or three people could compose a story together, but each student was expected to write his/her own copy of the collaborative story. Second, children were asked to be more conscious of what classmates were working on in writing workshop. Once a week in class sharing each author gave a brief, 2-minute retelling of her/his work in progress. Children in this session were encouraged to borrow ideas from classmates and to use them in their own writing. They began to see this as one way of collaborating, and the pejorative refrain, "that's copying!" vanished from the classroom. By honoring and legitimizing collaboration in writing workshop, I was giving in to what, in the past, had been a clearly stated need for many young writers. I realized that collaboration allowed writers time to talk about writing as they composed and that, for some, this was a valuable alternative to rehearsal and planning. It also provided a social context for the creation of texts in a jargon-free spontaneous manner.

I also re-examined the purpose of class sharing. I had thought of it as a time when an author could read a draft in progress or finished story to an audience of peers and get feedback in the form of questions from that audience. Yet, my research had indicated that authors in this context often felt like the bat reading his story to a bunch of mockingbirds. How to restructure class-sharing sessions remained a dilemma for me until Pamela finally shared her story.

"THE MAN WHO WAS LATE FOR DINNER"

Writing workshop was proceeding along nicely when Pamela, who had been working on her story for almost 3 months, first took the author's chair. The story describes the adventures of Bob Pomerance. Bob decided to have a party for the entire neighborhood, including both children and adults. For some reason, Bob did not tell the adults that children were invited. He wanted to keep this a secret so he spent most of the party shuttling back and forth between the children's and adults' rooms. He was forced to make an excuse each time he needed to leave a room. In a sense, Bob's party was really two secret parties going on at once. As the party was concluding, one of the parents asked Bob to come to dinner in 2 weeks. Bob accepted. On the appointed day he set out for his destination.

> Bob was outside walking to Ms. Karput's house. He walked for a very long time. Then he stopped. He said, "This isn't the right way." He turned around and started back. But that did no good either. Bob was LOST. He tried every way to go, but he was still lost. It was starting to get dark. The wind blew lightly against his face. The sky stood still. It looked like all there was in the

world was darkness. The sky seemed close to Bob. Bob rested against a stone. Then you know it! Bob fell asleep.

Bob woke up and walked into a small town and saw store signs lining both sides of the street. He began to visit each store. What was significant about each visit was that each store was owned or managed by an actual member of the class. Here are two of Bob's most notable visits: one to Alice's, who happened to be the most frequently consulted speller in the class, and the other to Christopher's, who had at that time published the most in writing workshop.

> He was walking down the street and he saw another store called Alice's Super Spelling. Bob went in. H-E-L-L-O," said Alice who was spelling her words. "Hello," said Bob.
> "W-H-A-T D-O Y-O-U W-A-N-T?"
> "Nothing. I am just looking around."
> "O-K-A-Y," said Alice.
> Bob said, "Do you have level nine?" [This is a reference to the 18-level spelling program used by the children in this class.]
> "Y-E-S W-E D-O. L-O-O-K I-N T-H-E B-A-C-K B-A-R-R-E-L."
> "Thank you," said Bob.
> "Y-O-U A-R-E W-E-L-C-O-M-E!" said Alice.
> Bob paid and left. Then he saw another store called Christopher's Books. Bob went inside. He looked at one of Christopher's books. He looked at the dedication page and saw that it was dedicated to Christopher. "Wait a minute," said Bob. "Didn't Christopher make this book? Yes. He did. It said on the cover." Bob asked Christopher, "Why did you dedicate this book to yourself?"
> "Oh, baycause deybee oar sew special!" (Oh, because they are so special!) said Christopher. Bob looked in all the books and the books were all dedicated to Christopher and they were all by Christopher. Bob decided to buy a book called The Man Who Was Late for Dinner.

With an intimate knowledge of her classmates, Pamela had created stores that had a certain ambiance or sold a particular product that was strangely appropriate to its owner. She had constructed places that legitimized even the most marginal members of the class, including her teachers! In all, Bob visited 24 stores. Finally, he reached the last one.

Suddenly he felt very tired and fell asleep. When he woke up, Bob was in his own house or what looked like his own house. It was his house. Bob thought that this was another weird thing that was happening to him again. He looked at the clock. It was 5:45. "I'd better hurry up or I'll be late." Because he had to go to dinner at 6:00. So he got ready and left. The end . . . but stay tuned for "The Man Who Was Late for Dinner, Part Two."

It is not clear just how late the man was or whether he ever reached his destination. It is clear, however, that he visited and shopped in each and every store. His journey was inclusive, leaving no one out. His quest seemed to be to participate, either by buying or just browsing in the world of each store, metaphorically in the world of each member of the class.

A Different Response

As Pamela read her story, the class listened with rapt attention. They then responded with questions and suggestions. I was struck by the intense laughter and playful energy that permeated the entire session:

Joe: What is that last store going to be?

Pamela: I haven't made it up. Jacob?

Jacob: I have an idea what it could be. It could be like Tutu's Tutu Store, YO-yo's YO-yo Store.

Darlene: I like being in your story and the part when Bob, he sees all the signs. I like that part.

Jacob: I think, like, the woman should say when he finally gets there, "Well, WHAT TOOK YOU SO LONG!" and that will be the end.

Pamela: Yeah, he'll get there and knock on the door and she'll say, "Well, Bob, what took you so long?"

Clyde: Then it will be like 10 minutes late.

Pamela: No, 10 minutes early.

Josh: It should all be a dream.

Clyde: Oh, yeah. Time has stopped.

Alice: Well, you could just make him think it was a dream, but then he reaches in his pocket and finds that diamond.

Pamela: Yeah, yeah. That's a good idea.

Alice: And he's gonna say, "What?"

Darlene: I have an idea. Everything that happens after the nap could be his dream, and then he could hear some noise, like

> a telephone call that canceled dinner till the next day. So
> . . . then the next day he could go to dinner and not get
> lost. Then that could be the end.
> *Pamela:* No, I'll make him get lost again, "The Man Who Was
> Late for Dinner, Part Two."

Early in the share, Darlene set an interesting tone by indicating that she liked being in Pamela's story. Her response affirmed at least one of Pamela's intentions for writing the piece in the first place: to include all members of the class. At this point, the class response mode changed dramatically. Instead of being outside the story and responding passively, members of the class actually got inside Pamela's story and responded to it like they were the actual writers. Nor was Pamela left out of this process of co-construction. In all, seven children, including Pamela, offered suggestions on how to change or end the story. Pamela came away from this class sharing feeling neither defensive nor misunderstood. Like the bat after he read his poem to the chipmunk, Pamela returned to her writing with the incentive to revise and compose more.

Understandings

In "The Man Who Was Late for Dinner" Pamela constructed a world that legitimized every member of a writing community. In the sharing session, the class acknowledged this and responded in a way that sustained Pamela and showed her the power of creating worlds through writing. The metaphor that Pamela had created, that of a world that included everyone, was embraced by other writers in the class. Clyde began to write a story entitled "The Man Who Was Late for Lunch," while Arthur and Nat collaborated on a tale about an imaginary land called "Slime World." Darlene, in her fictional story "I Hate Teachers and They Hate Me," used a setting much like the world of her own classroom, with characters who were undeniably her own classmates. Martin and Jacob began to write a story called "The Comedians," a comedy sketch that poked fun at the foibles of each member of the class.

In an end-of-the-year interview, Pamela described one way students collaborated on ideas and how these ideas propagated and spread in this writing workshop.

> Well, it sort of came back and forth because when I started my
> story, he was making a story called "The Man Who Was Five

Minutes Late" so I got some ideas from that and then he got
another idea from me and then he just did another version
except he was late for lunch.

Frank Smith (1988) contends that the metaphors we use in our lives as
teachers often shape the way we perceive children in the classroom. In
his view, metaphors are a way of structuring reality. Consequently,
using archaic or outdated metaphors in the classroom can in some
instances confine and limit our thinking about children and learning.
As I re-read Pamela's story and the transcript of her class sharing for
the tenth time, I realized that as a teacher I was not prepared to recognize new and important metaphors. Like the mockingbird, I was mired
in an expert point of view that prevented me from grasping not only
the metaphors in children's writings, but the intentions behind those
metaphors. Pamela had used fiction to create an inclusive world and,
by doing so, had invited the class to live in that world during sharing
sessions. Her metaphor, that of the mind as creator of worlds, was
powerful enough to be utilized by others in the classroom. As world
creators, the class brought a much more constructivistic attitude to the
writing process and to most response situations.

If I was to truly understand and respond honestly to the writing
of third graders as the class had to Pamela's story, I needed to discard
the metaphor on which I had relied for years and that restricted my
thinking. Supported by most language theory and research, this metaphor describes the brain as a processor of information. Language and
writing are methods of shunting information from one person to the
next. In writing workshop emerging writers use the personal narrative
as a way of communicating experience, and the primary goal is to write
in a clear, concise, detailed style about experience. With this metaphor
in mind, I programmed my students to respond to text from the point
of view of expert critical readers concerned with clarity, detail, voice,
and correctness. This point of view is what Smith complains about
when he asserts that schools attempt to produce secretaries instead of
authors.

A New Metaphor

Pamela and her inclusive world have led me to a different and more
powerful metaphor that is much more appropriate to the writing process and, over time, to the acquisition of literacy. The true power and
connective quality of writing became apparent to writers like Pamela
when they were permitted to engage in the construction of real or

imaginary worlds. In the context of our writing workshop, Pamela became an artist whose work, like all works of art, suggests a different imaginative world for her audience. She created a world that included her classmates. They, in turn, discovered the power of creating worlds like hers through writing and adopted her idea, even her metaphor. The connection occurred because the audience was thinking and listening to her story like writers or world creators, not like readers concerned with information and clarity.

Wells (1991) describes a model of literacy that is based on how readers and writers engage with written text. He suggests that to be fully literate, readers and writers must experience certain modes of engagement. The re-creational mode clearly supports the metaphor of mind as world creator.

> In calling this mode re-creational, I intend to capture the sense of engagement with the text as an end in itself, under-taken for the pleasure of constructing and exploring a world through words, one's own or those of another author. (p. 49)

Pamela and others in the class were clearly engaged with their writing in the re-creational mode. The playful tone and constructivist quality of recorded sharing sessions demonstrated that they took great pleasure in the creation and exploration of their worlds. More important, a writing culture had developed that used the same mode of engagement with written text, allowing its members to respond honestly and appropriately to the worlds created in those texts. Both audience and author were co-constructors in the fictive world of writing workshop.

The constructivistic and collaborative nature of conferences and class sharing also influenced those children who chose to write in genres other than fiction: personal narratives, poetry, and exposition. Recordings of these encounters show an empathetic audience willing to offer playful suggestions. Instead of deflecting them as often had happened in the past, authors were receptive. This receptivity invited even more suggestions, further strengthening the process of writer and audience composing, rather than critiquing, together.

There is an emotional component to teacher research, rarely mentioned in the expanding literature of the field, that helps explain why teachers do it. For 2 years I had been deeply embedded in the talk and the text of process writing in my classroom. My journey allowed me to listen more intently and read more carefully than ever before. It quieted the frenetic distractions of teaching and brought me much closer to the world of young writers. As my understanding of that world grew, so did my emotional attachment to it. In that world I came to respect and admire the integrity of all the children as they wrestled with the immense task of becoming literate writers. In 24 years of teaching, I had never grown so emotionally attached to a group of children as I did to this class.

Martin used a wonderful metaphor when asked to describe writing workshop: "It is kind of like a group of people writing at the same time in the same classroom. You can team up and it is kind of like a club." I remain indebted to these children for taking me on an exciting, rigorous journey that changed my theory and practice, gave me new knowledge about the writing process, showed me a new metaphor for learning, and offered me temporary membership in a fascinating club of writers.

CHAPTER 6

What's Real About Imagination?

ROXANNE PAPPENHEIMER

The imagination has been so debased that imagination—being imaginative—rather than the lynch-pin of our existence now stands as a synonym for something outside ourselves like science fiction or some new use for tangerine slices on raw pork chops—what an imaginative summer recipe—and Star Wars! so imaginative! The imagination has moved out of the realm of being our link, our most personal link, with our inner lives and the world outside that world.

—John Guare, 1990, pp. 33–34

Everyone uses the term *imagination*, but how many of us really know what imagination is? This chapter describes a brief foray into the imaginative worlds of two of my students, Mark and Sonia. Their imaginative worlds were not easy places to be. As a special educator of adolescent students with cognitive delays, I was trained in a way that featured a deficit model that permitted me to neatly package and dismiss certain words and actions and attribute them to my students' lower levels of cognition and their concrete thinking. My students' imaginings were widely labeled unrealistic or fantasy-based thinking, especially when compared with those of "normal" high school students.

To ignore a student's imagination may seem extreme to teachers in regular education. After all, students' imaginations are supposed to be nurtured in classrooms. Most young children's imaginations are naturally evident. They strike dramatic poses, conjure up imaginary friends, unearth evidence of the tooth fairy, and fervently believe in unicorns. Eventually, students learn to channel their imaginations toward more academic pursuits by authoring fictional stories, participating in drama, invoking analogies, taking perspectives, and visualizing future environments in which to participate.

Despite the centrality of this view of imagination in mainstream education, it did not seem to fit in my classroom. For example, when 15-year-old freshman Sonia confidently stated her desire to go to college, despite not being able to read at the second-grade level, comb her hair, or cross the street independently, I viewed her aspirations as problematic, as a hindrance that prevented her from seeing the world as it really is. Worried about her ability to form realistic goals, I helped her review her expectations. Together, we figured out the cost of college, previewed college texts, and attended a lecture at a local college. My hope was that she would independently conclude that her idea was not feasible. It wasn't until later—after I began to look at the role of imagination in my students' lives—that I fully appreciated Einstein's statement: "Imagination is more important than knowledge." This quotation provided me with a way of thinking about Sonia's aspirations. Did Sonia wish to attend college, or did she wish to imagine herself attending college? What could Sonia's desires mean to me, the teacher responsible for preparing her for adult life?

MY CLASSROOM

I teach in a public secondary school with nearly 1,700 students who come from 67 nations and speak 35 different languages. Sonia is from the Caribbean; Rick is from China; Mary is a Boston-area native. One middle-class 16-year-old has traveled abroad, while another supports his recently widowed mother and younger sister. Mark, who is legally blind, frequently injects his vast knowledge of drugs, sex, and violence into class discussions, while Ethan, who has pervasive developmental delays, prefers to retreat into his own thought processes.

These students are in my classroom because they've been labeled "developmentally delayed," "brain damaged," or "mentally retarded." Each struggles with academic and social tasks easily achieved by the vast majority of teenagers. Mark has trouble reading basic sight words; Ethan is still learning how to greet people; Sonia is unable to formulate her signature in cursive. Nearly everyone needs frequent "pep talks" on basic hygiene issues such as brushing teeth and taking regular showers.

As with other students with special needs, my students' school days are driven by an IEP, a document that lays out the goals, objectives, methodology, and time devoted to each skill taught. It is a document that sets measurable benchmarks based on the needs, strengths, and weaknesses of each student. My particular classroom is defined as "language-based" and "functional." Functional curriculum is considered meaningful and relevant when it prepares students for the realities of adult life. Assignments focus on specific survival skills such as maintaining a job, taking public transportation, writing grocery lists, managing a bank account, and making a phone call. Reading instruction is similarly devoted to deciphering medicine bottles, transit maps, television schedules, bills, and recipes. It is a pragmatic curriculum based in reality. There is no "once upon a time."

Given their need to review and break down information, my students have had little time to read the body of imaginative literature consumed by their peers throughout their school careers. For instance, in one discussion, I learned that no one had heard of *Alice in Wonderland* and nobody knew what a fable was. Few fairy tales could be recalled except those that had been viewed on video. Only one student read for pleasure outside of the classroom.

Although my students are exposed to the same social opportunities as other students at their high school, they often feel most comfortable staying together. They split up for many classes and play on different after-school sports teams, and yet they usually huddle together in the cafeteria during lunch time. They tend to rely on each other and their own immediate families for their primary social network outside of school. In this respect, they are socially isolated from the mainstream of teen life in the high school. Paradoxically, they do not necessarily identify one another as friends. If asked who their friends are, they often name someone they know from the cafeteria, an elective, or a club, or they describe a student, name unknown, who frequently greets them in the hallway. Despite efforts to pair them up in inclusive settings throughout the high school, involvement with mainstream students is not sustained. As a result, my students face a dilemma. In their quest to be in the same place as other teenagers, they often find themselves alone, ostracized, or, at best, "tolerated." In special education classes populated solely by students with special needs, my students are much more socially at ease, yet they fail to learn about the "teen scene" swirling about them in the rest of the school. Often, my students' curiosity about "what is currently cool" causes them to resort to the dubious solution of asking *me* to define it.

Because of my students' academic and social shortcomings, the casual observer easily can misinterpret who they are and what they can accomplish. Certainly, the labels "retarded" or "delayed" don't suggest the complexity of each student as an individual. In the program in which I teach, students enter as freshmen and stay with me for up to 8 years. Thus I have the opportunity to see in great depth and over the entire span of their adolescent development how remarkable these students are.

In the events I will describe below, my students came into contact with literature in a way rarely encountered in a functional, special education setting. Yet the journey through this encounter with "real" literature was fraught with difficulty and potential danger. As they entered the literary world of M. E. Kerr's *Night Kites* (1989), their imaginations were activated in ways that I had never seen in a regular education classroom. Their experience with literature outside the functional curriculum brought powerful changes, changes that challenged me as their teacher in ways I had not begun to anticipate. Through these events, Mark and Sonia taught me a great deal about their separate abilities to be imaginatively engaged as readers. These students provide the focal point of this chapter.

MARK

I first met Mark in the computer room at his elementary school. He was a large 13-year-old with an arresting appearance: His head was closely shaven except for a long "rat tail." He wore overly tight clothing, extemely thick glasses, and a hearing aid. Being legally blind, Mark had difficulty negotiating the classroom without his cane. When his teacher inquired about the cane's location, he deftly deferred responsibility for its whereabouts to his grandparents. During our conversation, he was articulate and motivated to be "cool." While expressing his eagerness to become part of the high school scene, he inquired about drugs, gangs, and graffiti. After hearing about our program at the high school, he expressed a desire to receive vocational support, get a job, and "make some change" so that he could buy CDs and electronic equipment.

Mark's teacher at the elementary school had requested that we explore the idea of Mark skipping a grade and moving to the high school. Due to health and motivational issues, Mark had been attending school only 20% of the time. The hope was that the vocational opportunities available at the high school would induce him to attend school. Although his teacher felt that a change in his program was necessary, she had concerns about Mark's safety at the high school. Mark freely expressed opinions without much awareness of whom he might be insulting. He felt that his racist, homophobic, and sexist comments were the norm, and lacked the understanding that some-one might become enraged enough to react violently.

The following year, Mark began attending high school regularly, proudly wearing a black leather jacket and eventually taking responsi-bility for bringing in his cane and maintaining his hearing aid. I soon learned that Mark's home life was complex. He lived with his grand-parents and up to three uncles at any given time. His grandmother, who struggled with health issues, seemed primarily responsible for Mark's well-being. Although Mark reported shouting, violence, and both alcohol and drug use in his family, there also was genuine love and care.

Mark came to the high school knowing that he wanted to be "cool." It almost seemed like he was performing a role. Difficulties prolifer-ated when he misinterpreted or overstated his role—especially with young women. His efforts to be involved were poignant reminders of the struggles that students with cognitive delays have in sustaining significant relationships with their peers. In his sophomore year, Mark announced his vocational goal to become Howard Stern's replacement as a radio talk show host. In his own words, Mark fully intended to "knock Howard Stern off the air." In order to accomplish this goal, Mark began to perfect a deliberately outrageous persona by inserting discus-sion of drugs, sex, violence, and graffiti into the classroom. To the amusement of his peers, he also rehearsed frequently his on-demand belching and farting techniques. Mark rejected interviews for jobs iden-tified by his vocational teacher, preferring instead to wait for his op-portunity to displace Howard Stern.

SONIA

While planning Sonia's transition to the high school, I attended a meeting at her elementary school. When I arrived, the students were still on the playground, and the teacher was providing supervision. The teacher pointed out Sonia, and I could not help noticing her unusual choice of clothes. Her elementary teacher explained that she had tried everything to help Sonia choose clothes less likely to result in ridicule by her peers. On any given day, Sonia might be wearing a mismatched symphony of textures and colors; sneakers with nylons or long under-wear; pants carefully ironed the night before, but put on backwards.

The staff also mentioned Sonia's determination to establish a social relationship with a male, a determination that frequently created a wake of angry and confused boys who were unable to deal with the intensity of any given encounter with Sonia. Her teachers were worried about her preoccupation and inability to assess the intentions of these young men. As if on cue, Sonia bounded over at that moment and joyfully announced, "He's looking at me." She tossed her head, smiling confidently. "Who is?" we asked. "That boy," she replied. We looked in the direction of her pointing finger. A staff member gently commented that all of the boys were playing basketball; their eyes were on the ball. Sonia's joy collapsed. Ignoring the teacher's efforts to call her back, she walked away after abruptly ending the conversation with a blank stare.

So, when Sonia entered the high school the following fall, I was already familiar with that blank stare. Equally apparent were her passive stance in class, her silence, and her easy tears. And yet, there were moments when she would comment happily about her latest boyfriend or excitedly recount the latest Rikki Lake or Power Rangers episode. Outside of the classroom, I had frequent glimpses of a fully animated Sonia running down the halls in pursuit of a young man who clearly was embarrassed or angered by the chase. In school, love notes frequently would flutter to the floor from her notebook. I would ask her if the person addressed in the note really was her boyfriend. Sonia would respond with tears and a blank stare, refusing to engage in conversation. Sometimes a frustrated young man would come to me asking for help. Sonia was calling his house four or five times a night, waking the entire family. Despite my interventions, she would find another red-faced young man for a relationship that existed only in her mind, announcing to his friends that she was his girlfriend. On two different occasions, male students asked to transfer out of class; they couldn't get Sonia to understand that they were only classmates.

In October of her sophomore year, Sonia accused a young man, Gary, known for his behavioral outbursts of demanding that she have sex with him. Both of these young people were about 16 years old at the time. In a meeting with administrators and a social worker, Gary was about to be disciplined despite his insistence that it had not happened. Since he was known as a troublemaker, it was easy not to believe him. As I looked at Sonia, however, I recognized her all-too-familiar confident pose. This prompted me to ask several questions: "Sonia, did Gary really say those words?" Sonia became very still. "Did those words come from his mouth into your ears? Or were the words in your mind?" No answer. "Did you hear the words or think the words?" Evident confusion began to erode her confident stance. Eventually Sonia responded, "The words were real. They were really in my head. I am not sure if I heard them." As we continued talking, we concluded that Gary had not propositioned her at all.

Early in Sonia's junior year, I arrived in the locker room after having been called by a concerned staff member. There I witnessed a dramatic and detailed telling of a romantic encounter that I later confirmed had not happened. Sonia was animated, her confidence evident, seemingly unaware of the snickering around her. It was a Sonia who was the diva of the ball, the lead actress with males swooning at her feet, the popular high school student with dates galore. After seeing me, she dejectedly climbed down from the bench and quietly finished dressing. She seemed to wilt. Although I was dismayed to see her joy and confidence gone, at the time I was pleased that Sonia knew enough about reality to change her behavior in my presence.

That year continued to be difficult as Sonia was asked to leave her homeroom and a dance class after not being able to control her amorous advances. One morning, Sonia's mother called the school. Sonia had been taken home, as usual, by a special needs van, but had not taken the elevator up to her apartment. Instead, she had decided to walk to her "boyfriend's" house by negotiating the streets independently—a potentially dangerous decision given her inability to cross streets safely. The next summer, she nearly lost her job in one of the summer programs, after a male co-worker complained about her persistence.

Over the years, I watched Sonia persevere; she held on to her reality of having boyfriends despite considerable intervention by staff and family members. She met weekly with a social worker; I consulted regularly with psychologists; we considered medication. In class, we discussed the difference between thinking about words in our head and hearing actual words being spoken. We talked about wishing for something versus something actually happening. We analyzed the nonverbal and verbal signs of sexual interest and disinterest by watching the characters on favorite TV programs; we read news articles on sexual harassment. We carefully defined the differences between a classmate, a peer, a friend, an acquaintance, and a romantic partner. Sonia was provided one-on-one staffing during the unstructured moments of the day. Behavioral contracts were written with the final—and often painful—consequence of dropping a class. Despite these efforts, Sonia remained unable to control her amorous advances.

A DILEMMA

By their junior year, I felt that I clearly had failed both Sonia and Mark. I had failed despite my design of a functional curriculum that provided vocational opportunities, that explicitly addressed behavioral issues, and that helped them differentiate reality from fantasy. I began to wonder what kind of functional curriculum would have a ghost of a chance, given the students' intensity in pursuing their unrealistic and, it seemed to me, self-defeating dreams.

But as I persisted in helping the students establish what I considered to be realistic goals, I also had a growing sense of uneasiness. There was something extremely judgmental and omnipotent in my stance. After all, I wouldn't necessarily dismiss an ambitious, talented high school student who aspired to become the next Howard Stern. Nor could I set aside my wondrous glimpse of a fully engaged, vibrant Sonia expounding in the locker room, pursuing a young man in the hallway, and rapturously writing love notes. I began to worry that my assumptions about the world might block my ability to see these students as individuals capable of envisioning their own futures. Each of them displayed a drive, an intensity that I wanted to transform, not extinguish. What parts of their visions should I listen to and work with, and what should I set aside? I realized that I did not know what to do. I felt as if there were no answers.

TEACHER AS LEARNER

In 1996, I had the pleasure of working with an intelligent and enthusiastic student teacher. Hired as an aide, Austin had decided to stay on for another year as a student teacher. In January, he announced his plans to read M. E. Kerr's adolescent novel, *Night Kites*, in class. I quickly read the book and immediately suspected that this venture might be a difficult one. I wondered how Sonia would handle the romantic scenes. Given Mark's homophobic comments, how would he respond to the gay character in the book? How would the students react to the scenes involving domestic disputes? Three of the students had limited decoding skills and were able to read only short paragraphs. Ethan had difficulty paying attention during any classroom discussion. How could he possibly remain focused enough to follow a book being read aloud with the rest of the class? I easily could anticipate that the students would have difficulty keeping track of the characters and places, would be confounded by complex sentences, and would be stunned by idioms. Additionally, I wondered how the time-consuming task of reading a complicated adolescent book would provide measurable progress as defined by the IEPs. These plans had been written to address functional academic skills within a strictly fixed period of time. I considered the challenge of explaining this departure from standard, well-accepted functional academic fare to parents, administrators, and Austin's academic program advisor. Nevertheless, as Austin and I discussed his ideas for teaching the book, I decide to quiet my reluctance and support his decision. I was confident that Austin would put in the necessary effort to prepare thoughtful lessons.

We ordered *Night Kites* from the Perkins School for the Blind's collection of Books on Tape to accommodate Mark, who struggled to see the print even in a large-print book. During the first week, Austin provided an introduction to novels in general. During the second week, visuals began to fill the room as the students learned how to negotiate a plethora of names, places, and changing relationships. A large chart with names and movable arrows was used to clarify the shifting relationships of the characters. In response to confusion over the idiom, "he jumped out of the car," Austin designed a model car out of cardboard and paper. The car was used to keep track of the particular scene in which the idiom appeared. The students were given the homework assignment of drawing pictures of individual characters. These portrayals were used to trace turns in the dialogue and to keep track of which characters were in various scenes in the book.

Each student eventually decided to choose his/her own character and read that character's words while engaged in role play. By Chapter 3, all of the students, with the exception of Ethan, had fully assumed the personalities of the book characters they had chosen to represent. For example, Sonia chose to read the part of Dill, a popular young teenager who was on the pom-pom team and had the status of being the narrator's girlfriend in the beginning chapters. Sonia was pleased with her role and took it very seriously. In fact, she insisted on remaining in character even when we weren't reading the book, as can be noted in the following transcript of a conversation that took place immediately before class:

> *Austin:* Can you get the door, Sonia?
> *Sonia:* (solemnly) I'm Dill now, Austin.
> *Austin:* Okay, you are Dill now. Thanks, Dill.
> *Sonia:* (giggle) Sometimes I have to remind you.

Her determination to stay in character is also evident in this conversation taped on the same day during reading class.

> *Austin:* What kind of hands does Dill have?
> *Sonia:* Square?
> *Austin:* (reading from book) Little square hands.
> *Sonia:* Little square hands. (incredulous tone) My hand doesn't
>   even look square.

Mark: How could your hand look square?
Austin: Are we talking about Dill's hands or Sonia's?
Sonia: (long pause) Dill.

Sonia remained so much in character as Dill that she became angry at both the characters in the book and the students who were reading those characters' parts. In the story, Dill's boyfriend becomes interested in another character, Niki. In one class session, Sonia became so outraged that she yelled at her classmate Mary, who was reading the part of Niki, a sexy, provocative character in the book, "Hey, you can't steal my boyfriend." During the rest of the period, Sonia sat hunched over in her chair and shot angry looks at her classmate. For days, Sonia felt a genuine loss in status.

While Sonia remained carefully in character, Mark was flexible in his ability to pirate any character whose immediate concerns related to his own. In addition to reading the part of a gay character who was dying of AIDS, Mark adeptly assumed his classmate Ethan's role as narrator by actively pursuing a relationship with Mary. Mark became angry with Ethan and pursued Mary by deliberately telling Ethan, "Back off—she's my girlfriend."

Other shifts occurred in the classroom social terrain as the book reading progressed. Within a week's time, nearly everyone was upset with everyone else. Emotions flared, and resolution was elusive because identities were constantly shifting and boundaries were few. Students were upset with not only the characters but with their classmates. They began arguing with one another, mixing up the fiction in the book with the reality of their lives. And yet, in the classroom, they had a more active interest in one another. Early mornings were filled with furtive glances and whispered gossip as they sat on a blue couch—away from the teacher. During class discussions, there was a frenetic eagerness to answer, to have their turn, to enter the text together.

By mid-March, after a series of particularly chaotic, confusing days, I began to consider whether we should stop reading *Night Kites*. Frustrated and tired, I arrived at a weekly BTRS meeting, which had not yet begun. A snack was being put onto the table while members straggled into the room. Exhausted and bewildered, I proclaimed that I "needed to do something" about my students' response to *Night Kites*.

To my surprise, my dismay was met with the group's full, intense attention. Those present listened and probed with a deep respect for the chaos that the students were creating. No one offered familiar prescriptive remarks that began with, "Have you tried . . . ?" My colleagues wanted to know more; they saw nothing to fix! And yet they saw the depth of the problems. Several members advised me to view the chaos as data and to think about it further with the group. After this meeting, I returned to my classroom with new possibilities; I no longer sought a "solution" to a "problem." While still concerned with the unexpected and deeply problematic nature of the students' response to literature, I began to observe, audiotape classroom discussions, keep field notes, and review transcripts.

CREATING THEIR OWN TEXT

The students began arriving earlier and earlier in the morning. They would appear with books in hand, sit at our meeting table, and ask to begin before the scheduled time. After a few weeks, they requested 4 more hours per week to read *Night Kites*. The audiotape version of the book arrived. The steady voice of the reader helped Mark and the rest of the students get from one page to the next. While the book tape was playing, the students carefully followed along. At times, they would become impatient with the teachers' inability to cue the tape to the right spot and excitedly would scan the text for words to support a point of view or answer a question. This normally passive group of students became engaged in animated, loud discussions. In fact, there was so much discussion that progress through the text was extremely slow. It was not unusual to cover one page during a 2-hour class. It was during this time that I brought in my own tape recorder and began to tape their conversations.

When Austin and I deliberately interrupted the students to inject the skill of turn taking, conversation would cease. Students would appear confused or stunned by our insistence on pragmatics while they were focusing on meaning. They began to use Austin and me in a different way. No longer were questions and comments addressed primarily to us. There was no waiting for the teacher's question. The teacher became participant and the students spoke freely, answering one another's questions, expounding on one another's ideas, creating their own understandings. They seemed to be claiming their own learning in a way I had not witnessed previously.

Two years after they finished reading *Night Kites*, I encountered a book by Jeffrey Wilhelm (1996) which makes the argument that teachers can help marginal students become motivated to read by helping them enter the book, by "being the book." The following passage seemed to capture what I had seen in my classroom:

> If reading is truly the producing of meaning, then all the materials of the curriculum become pre-texts, by which I mean an excuse or a reason to pursue personal inquiry and create personal meanings. If we are interested in student learning and transformation, then textbooks and stories become the texts that catalyze the real text that is the reader's response and new understanding. The questions and the answers will become those of the student and may be most fruitfully embedded and expressed through creative, artistic, and student-centered response "texts." (p. 10)

Austin and I learned to talk less and appreciate the students' bursts of intellectual activity. If the conversation became dynamic and my tape recorder was not already running, I quickly would turn it on. The students began to recognize this action and would exclaim in my absence, "Turn on the tape recorder. Roxanne would like to hear this." It was as if they could step out of their conversation, recognize that it had value, and anticipate my desire to learn with and from them.

Being the Book

As the days passed, it became more evident to me that the students were actively comparing their own lives with the events depicted in the novel. Yet the way they did this was sometimes so engaged as to be alarming. In the moments leading up to the following transcript, for example, the students had been listening to a section on the tape where Mr. Rudd, the narrator's father, angrily advances toward his son's bedroom. After the passage, the students requested that the book tape be shut off, and the conversation literally exploded as the students related personal accounts of family arguments complete with door slamming, yelling, and angry footsteps. Everyone was interrupting, agreeing, disagreeing, and adding a personal story. Mark, who had been waiting for a lull in the classroom conversation, finally gained the attention of his classmates and insisted that Austin act out the part of the angry father, Mr. Rudd.

> *Mark:* Well, would you act like Mr. Rudd right now?
> *Austin:* What do you mean?
> *Mark:* Well, right now. Right on the job. Can you do it?
> *Rick:* Act it out?
> *Mark:* Yeh.
> *Austin:* You mean you want me to make mad footsteps?
> *Mark:* Yeh.

> *Rick:* Boom . . . Boom . . . just . . . just . . . step your foot on the
>   floor.
> *Sonia:* Ow.
> *Austin:* Umm. . . . What else do you want me to do?
> *Mark:* Pretend you are coming right into your son's room . . .
>   and and and pretend Eric [the narrator] is like lying on the
>   bed and and you start yelling at him.
> *Austin:* Did that happen in the book?
> *Mark:* No. . . . No we don't know that yet. . . . But but pretend
>   that you are staring at him when you come into the room.
> *Austin:* Umm. Are you making a guess about what's going to
>   happen next?
> *Mark:* (hesitates) Yeh.
> *Austin:* How come you want to see an angry scene? You haven't
>   told us to act out any other scenes before.
> *Sonia:* Why this one?
> *Mark:* Because it is like emotion. So it is like a emotion scene . . .
>   where . . . you know . . . where somebody is making an
>   emotion . . . where they're mad . . . cuz the person won't go
>   somewhere with them.
> *Mary:* Maybe you had that experience in your life? Before?

Austin and I considered that his request might be a tactic to go "off-topic" in an attempt to discuss violence, one of Mark's favorite topics, and we tried to redirect the conversation. Mary and Sonia, however, assumed that his request to re-enact the scene was genuine; they asked him questions that got to the heart of his attempt to solve a problem by re-enactment, thereby possibly emancipating Mark to explore new possibilities. Mark eventually volunteered that he broke a police scanner, his prized electronic possession, during a loud disagreement with his grandfather. Mary and Sonia clearly had understood his intention to work out something in his own life.

The Role of Imagination

At about this time, Karen Gallas spoke in a seminar meeting about imagination. Karen stated that she was paying attention to her own imaginings and thinking about imagination as a tool in education. I remember that we all were so excited about her ideas that for a short time chaos reigned at the table. As the meeting continued, I had considerable difficulty focusing. I was too busy remapping my own classroom's topography and dealing with my anxiety. Was Mark's wish to be the next Howard Stern any different than my wish to hit the lottery—especially since I never actually buy lottery tickets? I again thought of Mark's request to act out the angry footsteps scene. Did it reveal the imaginative pursuit of a deeper understanding of family discord? Were both Mark and Sonia using characters in the book in the same way young children re-enact and understand events in their own lives? While I originally had thought that teaching decoding and comprehension skills was perhaps the best outcome I could expect from Austin's idea of reading the novel, both Sonia and Mark were demonstrating the power of a story to help us to imagine the possible and escape from the irrefutable past.

There were quieter, but no less dramatic, moments too. For instance, in field notes beginning in mid-March 1995, I noted Sonia's early morning entrance into the classroom, when she announced, "Look, I dressed like Dill today." And, indeed, she had. In playing the part of Dill, she had reconsidered her own unusual style of dressing. Despite her established history of dressing in a melange of cacophonous colors, she had the neat, preppie appearance of a pom-pom girl. I was amazed as I recalled all of the curriculum that I and other teachers had developed to help her with her appearance. Despite our expertise, we had not reached her. Dill had.

Sonia's conventional attire persisted throughout the 6 months we read the book. Afterwards, she shifted back to her own idiosyncratic style, but I observed over the next year that at least her repertoire of clothing styles had expanded because she would now observe what was outside of her and add new ways of dressing. On certain occasions she would dress in conventionally appropriate ways, explicitly telling me that she had found a look in a magazine or that she was dressing like a character in a book or movie.

I learned to appreciate the students' determination to use the book as their entry point into the dramatic and social world of high school students, a world that had always eluded them. It seemed as if I had found a strange and unexpected part of an answer to my original question: How could these students learn about social life if they could not be accepted successfully in the social world of the high school? The students had created an imagined yet real social world of their own through entering the book, a world with at least some of the features of the high school. Austin and I watched as *Night Kites* actually provided a setting where the students catapulted over the confines of their lives. This was exciting to them and to us, their teachers; but I was not ready to call it a real answer.

Possibilities

The process of "being the book" had opened up for our students some possibilities that we had not been able to provide within our functional curriculum. However, with students like these, some might ask, Is there any point to spending time on the traditional contents of language arts classes: the nature of authorship, characterization, plot, and other literary conventions and practices? I discovered that my students persisted, in spite of my instruction, in overruling conventional understandings of how a novel was put together, of what it "really" was. For them, characters were real people. At times, they were certain that Austin and I had written the book or that the characters might have influenced the author's plot. As rookies in the world of adolescent literature, the students came without much prior knowledge regarding authors and characters. For example, in the following transcript, Mark suggests that Erik, the narrator in *Night Kites*, could have consulted with the author regarding the plot of the story.

> *Mark:* But what if she [M. E. Kerr, the author] . . . I know but
> what if Erik and and Erik came up to her . . .
> *Austin:* Uh uh . . .
> *Mark:* M. E. Kerr.
> *Austin:* Okay. (deliberately)
> *Mark:* (conspiratorial tone) And said, "I want to write a story
> with a little twist in my brother on it."
> *Austin:* Um.
> *Mark:* (definitively) That's probably what happened.
> *Austin:* Are you saying that Erik Rudd is a real person? (silence)
> *Mark:* No reason not to. Well maybe there is. I don't know.
> *Rick:* Maybe maybe a make-up character.
> *Austin:* Well, Rick thinks maybe he is a made up character.
> What do you think, Sonia?
> *Sonia:* I think he is probably real. (interrupted)
> *Mark:* Maybe he's just an actor or something.

At the time, Austin and I were, once again, bewildered. Did Mark really envision a scenario in which Erik, the narrator, wrestled from M. E. Kerr the reins of authorship? What made my students wish to see the characters as authors of their own fate rather than fictitious figments of the author's imagination? We wondered whether Mark thought characters were actors, similar to television. I had assumed that

the students' failure to understand the place of both literary characters and authors was evidence of their disability. We had seen that they
were tremendously successful, given appropriate supports, at entering
the book. But what they didn't seem to have was the ability to pull
themselves out of the book, to look at the book as the creation of an
author, an object created for readers like them.

As the end of the school year approached, my students still discussed excitedly whether or not the characters were real people. They
decided to write letters to M. E. Kerr to ask about the characters (each
letter was answered by Kerr). They also planned to make suggestions
as to how the author might change the book. Sonia wrote stating that
she wanted to become pen pals with one of the characters.

Even though at the end of 6 months our students still seemed to
confuse fictional characters with real people—wishing to correspond with
both the author and the characters—I did see students use the text as
text. More important, however, was the "near distancing" that Mark
experienced. While nearly all the students remained with their adopted
character during our reading of *Night Kites*, Mark was the exception. At
first Mark had taken on Peter, the gay character, without knowing he
was gay. After learning that his character was gay and had AIDS, Mark
was hesitant to remain in character as often as did the other students.
As the character came into the classroom, we had multiple discussions
about being gay. As mentioned earlier, one of Mark's favorite targets was
gay people, so we had wondered how he would respond to this aspect of
the book. As expected, Mark's giggling, snickering, and rude remarks were
conspicuous. Austin and I consistently and assiduously sanctioned Mark
for these remarks, but they still continued.

However, as the months passed, and students grappled with the
nature of the author's creation, Mark tried desperately to understand
M. E. Kerr's motivation for including a gay character. In the transcript
above, Mark hypothesized that Erik, the narrator, asked M. E. Kerr, the
author, to include a story "with a twist" about his gay brother, Peter.
During the same class session, Mary presented her ideas about authorship. She reflected on the author's motivation to write about Peter and
the topic of AIDS. Unsolicited by the teacher, she offered her thoughts,
and, amazingly, Mark listened respectfully, seeming to consider things
from a more distanced place, escaping for the moment his discomfort.

Mary: Author likes writing these words . . . these things down.
Austin: What do you mean?
Mary: I think, I think she thinks about it in her life. Maybe she
    has experience with gay people or AIDS people before.

> *Austin:* That is interesting. Do you think she has to have experiences with gay people or people with AIDS in order to be able write about it well?
> *Mark:* Yeh.
> *Mary:* Yeh or no. You don't have to. You just need to be near people who got it.

What is significant about this transcript is what isn't there. There is none of the snickering, silliness, comments under the breath, or disrespectful name calling that Mark frequently interjected into prior conversations where AIDS was mentioned. A month later, Mark entered into a dialogue with Austin about a person with AIDS.

> *Austin:* I actually . . . on Saturday I heard a man with AIDS come to speak to a group I'm working with.
> *Mark:* What? And he was the speaker?
> *Austin:* He was the speaker. And he was talking about how his life has changed now that he has AIDS.
> *Mark:* (quietly) Wow. He even said he had AIDS too, Austin?
> *Austin:* Yes.
> *Mark:* Wow.
> *Austin:* He was very open about it. He came to speak to our group because he has AIDS. He wanted our group to learn about it.

Egan (1992), like many others, asserts that literature has the power to broaden our empathy for other humans: "By imaginatively feeling what it would be like to be other than oneself, one begins to develop a prerequisite for treating others with as much respect as one treats oneself" (p. 55). To take on a character's perspective is an imaginative act that may evoke empathy in the process. In Mark's case, as he came in contact with a character who was gay, and engaged in talk about the book in which that character resided, he temporarily transcended his former stance. He seemed at least occasionally to leverage his experience with a fictional character into responding differently to something in "real life."

Lessons Learned

So what could I, their teacher, assume that my students actually learned from this extended and often terrifying (from the teachers' perspective) experience? I'll focus only on Sonia and Mark. I've written about how Sonia was able to learn something about presenting herself to the world in conventional attire, something that we could not teach her with our functional curriculum and counseling. It was not a complete transformation; on many days, Sonia still looked strange. However, she did learn how to look outside herself and model her dress after other, more conventionally acceptable characters, both real and fictional. In addition, she began to reach out and participate in discussions in our classroom. Before we read *Night Kites*, Sonia would sit quietly in her seat during classroom discussions. In the year that followed, she excitedly participated in discussions that engaged her imagination: poetry, fiction—but not mathematics!

What about her problematic imagined love affairs? After *Night Kites*, she and I began to set time aside to read adolescent romance novels. As I read, her face became dreamy; at other times she could not stifle her giggles. She and I talked about her romantic feelings toward young men. This was new. The blank stares I previously had elicited became more infrequent. Over time, I have come to recognize that Sonia's pursuit of possibilities can be considered within the norm. Sonia's public imaginings are not so different from the private imaginings of most other students in the high school. One principal difference is that she articulates and acts upon her imaginings publicly. Perhaps Sonia simply needs to tell her story and have her story reflected back in the context of a novel. Once reflected, the reality and the fantasy as reality can begin to shift for Sonia.

Mark's beginning movements away from his homophobic stance are described above, but here I would like to relate a more striking outcome, more striking because it shows how these students' experience with literature can be brought back to their understanding of the functional curriculum and their place in the real world. As I described above, early in the reading of *Night Kites*, Mark commandeered the role of the narrator, Erik. As part of this identity he started to pursue Niki, Erik's girlfriend in the novel, by being verbally and physically suggestive to Mary, the student who was taking Niki's part in class. In spite of our attempts to curtail his advances, this became so problematic that Mary, with the support of the staff and her mother, decided to ask for a sexual harassment hearing available to her through the school. In the hearing she confronted Mark and told him what made her uncomfortable. She also told him to stop. With the help of the staff, Mark came to understand that there were consequences to his actions, that Mary did not want his advances, and that he had to step out of his imaginings, out of his character, and stop. After the hearing, he did stop harassing Mary. This episode left both Austin and me wondering whether our experiment with literature had overstimulated these students in ways that would not be useful to them and in fact might even be harmful.

A year later, I was working with Mark on his entrance into the workplace. Now 17, he had gotten a job and needed to become familiar with the employees' handbook. This included a section on sexual harassment in the workplace. For teachers of students with developmental disabilities who are heading, we hope, for successful vocational placements, this is an area that evokes great concern. If a student does not understand the requirements of the workplace in areas such as sexual harassment, the result can be much worse than termination from the job. As I read through the manual with Mark, I could see that he understood it. He explicitly drew on his experience with *Night Kites* and the terrible episode that it evoked; he anticipated the contents of the policy before we had even read all the way through it. He stated his desire to be "respectful of the ladies." I knew that he actually had a base of social experience to draw from and that he would remember and understand this in a way that he could not have if we had approached the topic only through the functional curriculum.

CONCLUSION

Night Kites served as the catalyst for Sonia and Mark to rehearse their stories and create an imaginative space in which they and their classmates were integrated into a more accepting world that included the novel's characters and author as full participants. Although I initially thought that these students "didn't get" literature, I now marvel at their intuitive ability to satisfy personal needs and purposes by engaging with literature. Sonia and Mark used their imaginative powers to look beyond the actual and demand an alternative—a way out of the restrictive nature of their lives. When Jeffrey Wilhelm, author of *You Gotta BE the Book* (1996), interviewed highly engaged readers, he noted that

> Readers who successfully entered a story world began to make moves to relate to characters and see the story world. They noticed cues for creating and sustaining a "secondary world" in their minds as they read. They created characters and felt emotions in relation to character activities and problems. Quite often, the readers would become a presence in the story world, and begin to move around in that world or manipulate it in some way. In this way they would project themselves and their real-world knowledge into the story world. [They] evoked a complete story world, and at this point the virtual world of the story had intense and comprehensive reality for them. (p. 56)

Amazingly, the dynamic engagement of the students in my room easily could fit Wilhelm's description of what successful readers do. In that sense, my students are highly successful "readers" who, nevertheless, have difficulty with decoding and comprehension skills. There is, however, another major difference. In direct contrast to the students in Wilhelm's study, who were prompted to reveal their thoughts when engaged in a book, my students did not have the social awareness to keep their ideas private as they read. In fact, one of Wilhelm's students actually was reluctant to share her thoughts, stating that she felt that teachers were not interested in hearing how students go "underground" with their experiences as readers (p. 31). My students obviously did not have that inhibition. Not only did they articulate their notions, but they also sustained a public imaginary quest to uphold a "secondary world" while reading *Night Kites*.

After completing *Night Kites*, the students in my classroom pursued even more time to read. Their faces would soften as I read a poem; they savored newly comprehended metaphors; they gleefully awaited meeting new literary characters. These were truly amazing feats considering that these learners are labeled as concrete thinkers unable to generalize, synthesize, or perform other high levels of abstract thought. And yet, adolescent literature, with all its varied and steamy plots, provided them a way to do just that. It allowed them to reflect on their experience and meaning making by providing them the opportunity to imaginatively negotiate their way through the high school scene.

Within the context of my classroom, my role of teacher has changed. I believe that functional curriculum, which might be regarded as a factual narrative, needs to be reconsidered and taught in such a way as to engage imaginative processes. Instead of looking at reading in purely functional terms, as a means to derive literal meaning from texts or learn about life skills, reading should be considered as a site for unique human beings to engage in imaginative rehearsals that serve their own paths of development. I now know that the stories of others are essential in encouraging students to write their own stories and determine their own goals.

Still, I am unable to conclude this chapter gracefully. Questions remain: How does the ability to use one's imagination shape learning? When should unreliable images of reality be honored as a rehearsal of imaginary ideas? When do these unreliable images promote false hopes for the impossible and the outrageous? And how can we best use the power that imagination obviously holds to further our students' learning? While these questions and many more remain, I am in awe of the power of imagination. As Ursula LeGuin (1989) writes:

Only imagination can get us out of the bind of the eternal present, inventing or hypothesizing or pretending or discovering a way that reason can then follow into an infinity of options, a clue through the labyrinth of choice, a golden string, the story, leading us to the freedom that is properly human, the freedom open to those whose minds can accept unreality. (p. 45)

My students agree.

CHAPTER 7

Mainstreaming: Entering Another Classroom's Culture

Susan Black-Donellan

Over the past 25 years, much has happened to protect—and extend—
the rights of children who have special educational needs, particularly
their right to have access to the general curriculum, to study the same
things that regular education students study, and to share in the regular educational setting.

In 1975, the federal government passed PL 94-142, called the
Education for All Handicapped Children Act, which entitles students
with disabilities to a "free appropriate education." The most recently
amended version of this law is called the Individuals with Disabilities Act, one of whose stipulations is that all students have a right
to be educated in the "least restrictive environment." In Massachusetts the phrase used to describe this right of special needs students
is "access to the general curriculum." That is, students may leave
the specialized small-group setting and be integrated into the larger-
group setting of a regular classroom, which is considered to be less
restrictive.

"Mainstreaming," as this practice is called, requires schools to integrate special education students into regular education classrooms
for some part of their school day. Most special education programs are
designed around small-group settings. Mainstreamed students thus
must leave this familiar setting to go into large regular classrooms. As
many teachers and administrators have learned, this is a major and
complicated task.

LEARNING FROM STUDENTS

As a special educator who entered the field in the 1970s, I enthusiastically embraced the concept of mainstreaming and strongly advocated having special needs students integrated as much as possible into "regular" classrooms. In fact, at one point, I nearly alienated myself from some regular education teachers due to my zeal to mainstream my students with behavioral disorders. In my role of mainstreaming advocate, I spent a considerable amount of time negotiating mainstreaming with both teachers and students.

However, even I, committed as I was, could not fail to notice that students did not go gladly into this new, "less restrictive" environment. A special needs student begins mainstreaming only when the teacher assesses that that child is ready. Yet my students, when I determined that one of them was ready, were often reluctant to leave the special needs classroom to go to the regular class for the designated mainstreaming period. I had to develop a whole repertoire of incentives in order to convince them. I exhorted them in various ways. I told them that mainstreaming was important for them. They said it wasn't. I told them their goal was to be in the mainstream. They told me they didn't want to go. I told them that I knew what was best for them. They said that this was not it.

In the face of their resistance, I persisted. In the mid-1990s, I joined the BTRS, where I was encouraged by other teachers to think about aspects of my students and my teaching that puzzled or perplexed me. The group carried out research on such puzzles, as described in other chapters of this book. One of the topics we discussed at our meetings was classroom discourse and the different ways it influenced the social reality of classrooms. We read some of James Gee's work and became familiar with his idea of discourse: "a socially accepted association among ways of using language, of thinking and of acting that can be used to identify oneself as a member of a socially meaningful group or 'social network'" (Gee, 1989c, p. 1). Based on our reading of Gee, Cazden, and others, we developed our ideas about our own classrooms, particularly ideas about the unique discourse of each class.

For me, this material had a special significance. I have always believed that the classroom community has a strong impact on student learning and so must be carefully shaped by the teacher. Each classroom has a unique culture consisting of implicit and explicit rules. We develop symbols and language as a community; we construct our meanings together; we come to know one another as individuals as we become a cohesive group. To become a member of the classroom community, the child must understand both the stated and implied cultural norms of the community.

For example, my practice of alerting a child to his misbehavior would involve a nonthreatening but clear statement: "That's a 'reminder.'" I intended this statement to correct the behavior neutrally and not to personally threaten the child. Reminders were cumulative. Once a student received three reminders in a given period, he/she was sent to a "time out" area. Students also could earn points for lack of reminders. In this classroom, the simple three-word statement "that's a reminder" was really a symbol that stood for a whole system of practices related to student behavior and discipline. Students internalized these as they became members of our classroom culture. The statement "that's a reminder" was part of our classroom discourse and would not be readily understood by someone outside our community. There are many examples of this kind of learning in every classroom. The children who belong to the community know and understand the language and the culture.

After reading Gee's work on discourse and identity, and talking with my colleagues in the BTRS, I began to formulate new questions about my students. When they participate in the mainstreaming process, the special needs students are in the particularly difficult position of having to learn more than one classroom discourse. If my students are learning the discourse of the mainstream class with only a limited amount of time in such classroom, aren't they engaged in a complex learning process? Do the mainstreamed special needs students become, in some way, bicultural? If so, what does that say about our assumptions regarding their overall learning ability? They must be doing some extraordinary learning. I wanted to know how they did this, how they internalized the information, and, as their classroom teacher, how I could incorporate this learning process into my classroom practices.

With the seminar's help, I began to explore my students' encounters with the discourse of mainstream. My specific questions concerned what happened when they journeyed outside our own environment, with the routines and symbols they all understood well? How did they learn to interpret the discourse of the mainstream classrooms?

Looking back, my enthusiastic expectations seem astonishing. I did not, in fact, discover extraordinary learning. Rather, to my dismay, I discovered problems. Through my students' reports on their experiences, I was exposed to intricacies of mainstreaming to which I previously had been blind. In what follows, I will describe what I found and how I now understand it.

The Setting

This story begins with a special education class consisting of 4 first-grade students, 3 second-grade students, a teaching assistant, and myself. The learning problems of the individual students in this class varied, thus creating a fairly diverse group. Generally, special needs classrooms are designed to serve students with one predominant disability, such as a behavior disorders class or a learning disabilities class. A substantially separate or self-contained classroom such as mine usually is considered to be the most restrictive classroom setting within a public school. Children are assigned to such classes because the severity of their learning difficulties requires that they receive individualized instruction and specialized teaching techniques. Although they also are assigned to a certain grade-level regular class for the purpose of mainstreaming, the special needs class remains their homeroom.

The school was a culturally diverse K–3 school. It had the atmosphere of a neighborhood school with a tightknit sense of community. The class size averaged 22 students. For the most part, the teachers believed in the benefits of mainstreaming and welcomed the special needs students into their classes.

The Question

Members of the BTRS use a number of different research methods. Some have spent many months observing in a classroom, either tape-recording or just taking field notes. Others have asked students to carry out tasks and have analyzed the resulting student work. I decided on a direct approach. I got a tape recorder and interviewed the children. Because my workday did not allow me to follow all students into their mainstreaming classrooms, and because I could not interview each child separately, I interviewed them together.

I audiotaped their talk and then transcribed it. I brought the transcripts to the weekly seminar meetings, where we listened to and discussed the transcripts. At first the tapes seemed unrevealing. But over time and through discussions, we were able to hear what the students were telling us. What I learned about mainstreaming really came from listening to the students with my colleagues in the BTRS. What I learned was not what I thought I was going to learn, and not what I thought I knew already.

What I Found: The Children's View

The general response from my students was that they did not like to go to the mainstream classrooms. Believing as I did that mainstreaming is the crux of the special needs students' program, I was distressed by their attitude. Naturally I wanted to know more. (All the names used in this chapter are pseudonyms, except that of Steve Griffin, who is a member of BTRS and gave permission for his name to be used.)

Lacking Social Knowledge in Gym. Often, gym class is one of the first classes students are mainstreamed into since it does not require academic skills. This was the idea with Chuck, a second grader. Not only was Chuck physically fit but he also was well liked by his peers and had always impressed me with his good sportsmanship. I often would use Chuck's cooperative behavior as a positive example for the rest of the class. In spite of these advantages, Chuck found playing games hard.

Chuck had been placed in my special education class because of a severe learning disability, resulting in a need for intensive individualized instruction. He had, for the 2 previous years, received special education services in the resource room, yet he had attained only beginning first-grade reading skills. Teaching Chuck required using many specialized methods.

Yet he was physically fit, well coordinated, cooperative, and even tempered. Why would gym class be hard? What information does a child need in order to be competent at playing games? Chuck explains below, but his words alone do not convey the anguished feeling and resigned tone heard in the tape itself.

> *Teacher:* How about you, Chuck? Do you like going to Steve
>   Griffin's classroom?
> *Chuck:* (shakes head)
> *Teacher:* No?
> *Chuck:* Because (mumbles) . . . the gym (mumbles)
> *Teacher:* I'm sorry I didn't hear you.
> *Chuck:* Gym. It's hard
> *Teacher:* Gym is hard?
> *Chuck:* Yeah (mumbles) playing the games.
> *Teacher:* Mm-hmm
> *Chuck:* And (speaks softly and sighs) that's it.

The games in the gym class are generally team games. They are not as structured as academic subjects. Students are bombarded with multiple levels of information. First there is understanding the directives as well as the style of the teacher. Then there is learning the explicit and implicit rules. Next there is knowing the style and temperament of teammates and opponents: who the strong players are, the weak players, the fair players, and the unfair players. Finally, there is becoming accustomed to the physical space. One often must glean information through participation and observation. The dynamics of playing team games go beyond simply knowing the rules of the game. The children who are in a classroom community full-time learn implicit information about one another. Chuck, a child who visited this class for only a part of each day, lacked a wealth of information, which put him at a disadvantage and must have created some discomfort. It must have been exhausting. Yet gym is the period that commonly is recommended as the starting point for mainstreaming of the able-bodied student. For Chuck, being physically able and well liked did not guarantee a successful mainstream experience.

Different Expressions, Different Meanings. Earl also expressed lack of enthusiasm for mainstreaming. Earl was referred to the special education class because of a severe language disability, which made communication quite difficult for him. He often could not find the word he wanted or used words out of context or mispronounced them. In order to compensate for his difficulty, Earl frequently acted as if he did understand when he didn't at all.

Mr. Jones was the teacher of the first-grade class to which my first graders were mainstreamed. Although I saw Mr. Jones as very accommodating, my other students too expressed insecurities about being there. I wondered why, and started to consider the nature of the discourse practices that were common in his classroom. Mr. Jones's style involved frequent interjections of humor. For the learning-disabled student, this posed a challenge of interpretation. For example, in telling Earl to sit down, Mr. Jones might say, "Earl, ze bottom . . . sit on it." Like my use of the phrase "that's a reminder," his warnings to students were indirect and must come to be understood by becoming a member of the classroom. He was telling Earl in a lighthearted way to sit down. The full-time members of the class learned to understand and appreciate Mr. Jones's humor through frequent exposure. The special needs students just did not understand and consequently were probably confused. Earl is language disabled. How could he possibly process this? What happens when he does not sit down because he does not know he was told to sit down? Is he seen as defiant? Earl often would compensate for the inability to process language with bravado. So, he could come across as defiantly refusing a request when in fact he just did not have a clue as to what he had been asked to do.

Mr. Jones, as a teacher of 25 first-grade students, did not have the time to stop and determine whether the special needs students had sufficiently processed each simple request. Often, special needs students are acutely aware of tone and will rely on tone to determine content. The difference between my tone and Mr. Jones's tone, coupled with my students not fully understanding the discourse, I believe, resulted in the anxiety they experienced. Again, this comes from their not being members of the culture. Their lack of constant participation in this community meant that they could not adapt to the differences in the teacher's style, which was a part of this community. They could only guess at what was acceptable and hope that they conformed to the norms. When I questioned them as to how they knew what was the right thing to do in Mr. Jones's class, they said, "If you didn't get yelled at, you did the right thing." This is the kind of anxiety these children experienced in the "least restrictive setting."

Social Language and Peer Interaction. Ian experienced a range of special needs relating to his learning difficulties, which included limitations in social skills. Ian saw things from a different perspective. Much of his program was devoted to learning appropriate interactions with both peers and adults. Ian had achieved success in this area within our community, but I was particularly disturbed by his report of being in the mainstream. His interpretation of his mainstream experience was highly critical. Ian described how for him entering the mainstream class was an alienating experience.

> *Teacher:* Okay. Ian?
> *Ian:* I don't like it.
> *Teacher:* You don't like it either?
> *Ian:* It feels like that class doesn't pay attention to you. Doesn't like—'cause they always go like right next to you and say, "Can I play with you?" and then they ask again and again and again.
> *Teacher:* So you find that you are not like a part of the class?
> *Ian:* I like it better up here, a lot way better.

The exasperated and discouraged tone of Ian's response was striking. The phrase "again and again and again" seems to indicate that the peer relationships do not get beyond the introductory phase. I started to think about how children talk with one another after relationships are successfully formed. When children are friends, it is natural for them to play with one another. The formality of initiating play with a request becomes obsolete. The requests were significant for Ian because, I believe, they were a reminder to him that he was not a regular member of the community. The students of the mainstream class did not perceive the continuity of Ian's presence among them. Ian also commented, "That class doesn't pay attention to you." Understandably, Ian's attendance in the mainstream class was not as significant to the regular class students as it was to him. For the mainstream students, their routine would continue whether or not Ian was with them. For Ian, it was a significant event. His world had changed. He was in unfamiliar territory. He wanted to continue his ongoing work on social skills. But how do you do that if nobody is paying attention? Ian's tone as well as his words express his sense that going to the mainstream class was an alienating experience for him.

Missing a Frame of Reference. Earl here explains one aspect of what he perceives as different about Mr. Jones's class. His comments illuminate how the mainstreamed student lacks an accurate frame of reference to gauge the routine of the classroom experiences. Earl's concerns regarding the regular education class focus on "special things" happening.

> *Teacher:* What about you, Earl? Do you like to go to Mr. Jones's room?
> *Earl:* 'Cause it is not fun.
> *Teacher:* It is not fun?
> *Earl:* It's only fun if it is indoor recess and we get to pick.
> *Teacher:* Is it fun in this class?
> *Earl:* Yeah.
> *Teacher:* Why is it fun in this class?
> *Earl:* 'Cause we get to do fun things and special . . .
> *Teacher:* Mr. Jones doesn't do special things in the class?
> *Earl:* Not for us. That's why I don't like to go there.

Earl's response seems to point to many issues. Earl stated that Mr. Jones did not do special things for "us." He clearly saw himself and his special needs classmates as a separate entity. He did not identify the group as part of Mr. Jones's class. He, in fact, believed that special things happened outside of the time he spent in the classroom. Earl almost suggested that mainstreaming had a discriminatory component. However, given that he was with the class only on a limited basis, he did not have an accurate frame of reference from which to determine what was special. Perhaps, he was, in fact, missing the "fun things" or maybe he did participate in the fun things but was unaware of it because he did not have the rest of the day by which to measure what was mundane and what was special.

The second-grade students were mainstreamed to Steve Griffin's class. Steve Griffin is also a member of the BTRS. From our group meetings, I was more aware of what was happening in his classroom, and could accurately see how much my students' interpretation of events suffered from lack of a frame of reference and from lack of membership in the culture of his classroom.

Steve Griffin was researching sharing time in his classroom. As described elsewhere in this volume, the students were progressively redesigning the format for sharing time. Steve Griffin saw this process as unique to his classroom and therefore as part of the culture. We were both interested in how my students would interpret what was happening. This seemed to Steve and me a clear example of an event where my students were not part of the everyday occurrences. We decided that my students would observe rather than actually participate in sharing time since we expected it to be difficult for them to figure out at first. We saw this as a wonderful opportunity to follow my students' thinking.

John's report on sharing time in Steve Griffin's classroom shed some light on how special needs students frequently determine, however inaccurately, the hidden structures and routines of the regular classroom.

> *Teacher:* Okay you know what I was wondering about is, is Steve
>   Griffin's share [sharing time] like our share or is it different?
> *Chuck:* Kinda different.
> *John:* It's different.
> *Teacher:* Let John answer this question. Why is it different,
>   John?
> *John:* 'Cause we don't share like, um, how ya show . . . Take,
>   um, like toys to school but we don't [take] toys to school
>   and like up here 'cause we had a different one like book
>   share. But kids read books and they take time to um know it
>   and next sometimes they . . . Steve Griffin brings in the
>   camera, . . . they um have the story in their head.
> *Teacher:* Okay so they already know the story before sharing
>   time.

John: They don't have to be books.
Teacher: They don't have to be books?
John: 'Cause, um they took practice doing something.
Teacher: They practice the story before they do share?
John: Then they make up the stories and then they practice it.
Teacher: And they do share?
John: Yeah. They do it.

Their perceptions, while thoughtful, were quite inaccurate. Given the information that I had, I was baffled by my students' remarks. I had to double check with Steve Griffin. He assured me that there were no rehearsals or text involved. The reality of what was happening during this sharing time was that the students were creating fictitious stories, what they referred to as "I need people stories" (see Chapter 2).

John's interpretation of sharing time is similar to the way Earl interpreted the "special things" in Mr. Jones's class, in that John thought significant events were occurring while he was not there. John took it one step further and deduced, however incorrectly, what occurred while he was not there. John, in effect, filled in the gaps for himself. He did not know what to do with the fact that Steve Griffin was videotaping on this particular day. Probably John missed Steve's explanation of the camera. John tried to create a reason for the camera but somehow he could not quite place it. He was convinced it meant something.

John was placed in the special needs class so that he could receive help with his slow learning process. John often needed to have information presented to him slowly and repeatedly. Here he found himself having to understand something for which he was not fully informed so he created his own information. One wonders how often we are unable to fully inform the special education student about the meaning and nature of events in the regular classroom. How often do they have to rely on their own interpretations?

These two examples where a student clearly showed the lack of a frame of reference led me to wonder about the general contrasts my students observed in the two settings, so I asked them about differences. I believe that the strength of their responses also indicates a heightened, and perhaps exaggerated, perception of the contrast between the different settings. These are examples of what they felt to be the differences between the mainstream class and our class.

Robert: Well, in Steve Griffin's class, you don't get any free
    choice.
Teacher: What else, John?

John: If you want to play with the computer while he is talking, you can't play with the computer until after the next date.
Teacher: Okay, Linda?
Linda: In Mr. Jones's class it just like, um, they aren't even as big a library like ours, it's only a tiny library. They only have two seats.
Teacher: Hm,hm.
Linda: And also block corner and (goes into a lengthy description of the physical space).
Ian: Well, there the classrooms have boards that are bigger, like that are about the same size as about half of the part of the walls in this room.
Earl: Yeah, we have to act different 'cause he [garbled] then we go to the back table, our group, back table, and then everybody looks at you—you're stupid—us [garbled].

Some might wonder how much of the students' difficulty in verbalizing the differences is based in their special needs. Certainly the students' learning difficulties played a role in their observations. The responses of the students reflect their special needs. Robert stated that there was not as much free time in Steve Griffin's class. Robert's main disability was behavioral. He depended on free time as an outlet. John, on the other hand, identified a rule he knew well. Since John learned best concretely and through rote, his focus was on what he had practiced.

Behavior issues compounded Linda's learning problem. She focused on the various sections of the room as being different. She used the purposes of the different areas as a source of control. Ian, who was highly distractable, noticed the size difference, particularly the boards. Most likely he had a sense of containment in the small special education class, which he did not experience in the mainstream. Earl, who was quite sensitive, responded at an emotional level. He felt they had to act differently. Again Earl referred to his special education classmates as "we" and "us." He also expressed his sensitivity at being looked at and being "stupid."

MORE QUESTIONS

Although the students' learning difficulties are a factor, I now think that the process of mainstreaming would be difficult for any student when considered from the perspective of classroom culture. We are asking students to act as if they belong to a culture that is relatively unfamiliar. Their special needs only exacerbate what would naturally be difficult. Any child placed in a setting other than that to which he/she has grown accustomed would experience a sense of difference. I wonder why we expect special needs students to be so adaptable.

This study provided me with many insights as well as more questions to explore. As I listened to the tapes and studied the transcripts, I found that the transmission of the classroom culture is intricately woven into the fabric of the ongoing dialogue between the students and the teacher. The mainstreamed student enters in the middle of the conversation. As adults we can all identify with the feeling of entering in the middle of an ongoing event. We try to determine what has gone on from what is going on in such a way that we keep up with what continues to go on. It is no small feat. Yet this appears to be what we expect from special needs students when they are mainstreamed. To compound the situation, they leave before the conversation has come to an end. Even in the best of mainstreaming situations, it is impossible to keep a student abreast of what goes on in one classroom. So in one way or another the special needs student who participates in the mainstream experience is always at a disadvantage. Does this not contribute to the child's already acknowledged disadvantage?

Encouraging the special needs student to participate in mainstreaming, to some degree, is degrading to the special needs class. In effect, the child is being given the message that this class, where he/she is competent in the discourse, is not the ideal class. The ideal class is the one in which he/she feels out of place or, in Earl's word, "stupid." Does this not compound the students' already low self-esteem? The place where they can be competent is the "less than" community. It seems to me now to pose a dilemma: Children should strive to be out of the special class where they are competent so that they can be in the mainstream where they are incompetent. Why are we so uncomfortable about the classes where the students are comfortable? Isn't comfort an important ingredient of a quality public education?

As I recall the many special needs students I have worked with, I cannot recall a single one who requested to be mainstreamed. It was my enthusiasm for mainstreaming that was propelling them. Now I wonder, did they know what I did not recognize? Maybe. Of course, if we wait for students' requests, there may not be too much education going on. Still, I think that these children have a valid point, and they have taught me something. There are many theoretical bases for mainstreaming, but many of those theories are based on the adult's perception of the child's experience.

We, as adults, have an obligation to determine what is in the best interest of the child; this is our job. One of the greatest benefits of this study is that it has helped me see with the child's eyes, listen with the child's ears, and feel with the child's heart. I question whether the students feel as excluded in their special education classrooms as we adults are apt to think. Which is more inclusive: to be learning in an environment where one's needs are closely attended to and generally met, or an environment where one is a marginal member of the community and one's ability to compete is impaired? I now think more carefully about just what "least restrictive" means for young learners.

CHAPTER 8

"Look, Karen, I'm Running Like Jello": Imagination as a Question, a Topic, a Tool for Literacy Research and Learning

KAREN GALLAS

Emily is sitting alone at a table with one of her ants in her hand. She is talking to the ant, asking it questions: "Do you have anything else to say?" She puts her head close to the ant and listens. Later she explains that the ant has been telling her that she's 10 years old, and her birthday is August 2nd, and it's a her. She shows me how she wrote that information on a piece of paper. (Field Notes: September 22, 1995)

Emily was the first child I taught who, at 6, had quite plainly begun her life work. Emily was a scientist, and it is quite possible she was born that way because she was the only 6-year-old I have known whose life revolved around a desire to immerse herself exclusively in the study of the natural world. In Emily's case, her chief fascination was with insects, most especially ants. During the year I taught her, in fine weather she spent all of her outdoor time pursuing insects, capturing them, and making containers to keep them in so that she could take them home with her for further observation. As a collector, she was never without plastic baggies, and any crawling thing was scooped up and put in her cubby for later study. She drew the insects and bugs she collected, wrote about them avidly, and offered a wealth of information about most of

An earlier version of this chapter first appeared as "Look, Karen, I'm Running Like Jello: Imagination as a Question, a Topic, a Tool for Literacy Research and Learning" by Karen Gallas in *Research in the Teaching of English*, vol. 35, no. 4. Copyright © 2001 by the National Council of Teachers of English. Reprinted by permission.

them to anyone who was interested. She was not, however, a child who ever chose to read a fiction book or listen to a fiction story. She did not involve herself in dramatic play unless I asked her to do so. She insisted at home on being read only nonfiction, although her parents made valiant attempts to read fiction with her. If left to herself, her interests in life were exclusively in natural science and/or things that were "real." I was surprised, therefore, to find out early in the school year that Emily believed she could talk to insects (and who am I to say she couldn't). Often at recess, and sometimes in the classroom, she could be seen walking around engaged in serious conversation with whatever poor creature she had happened upon.

At the time I taught Emily I was beginning my third year of inquiry into the subject of imagination and the role it plays in early literacy, and she provided a unique example of the workings of imagination as it interfaced with a specific discipline. Yet Emily was just one child among many who were playing out their imaginative lives in plain view of anyone who cared to watch. This chapter places the imaginative work of Emily and many other children into a framework that attempts to focus attention on the role of imagination in literacy learning. It will describe how my questions about imagination emerged, although it will not claim to have answered those questions.

I will propose three ways in which I believe imagination is linked to discourse acquisition and forms a cornerstone of the literacy process for students of all ages, presenting data that focus on the issues of identity, discourse appropriation, and what I call "authoring." In each of these areas the development of my theoretical structure will be laid out chronologically so that the reader can see the recursive way in which my process as a teacher researcher changed my practice, which in turn changed my theoretical framework, which again changed my process as a teacher researcher, and so on.

My purpose in pursuing this chronological process is to try to make tangible the role of imagination as I have seen it working in my primary classroom, and to open up for discussion the necessity, in fact what I believe to be the imperative, of studying more closely the imaginative work of literacy learners. It would, however, be the height of hubris for me to make the claim that by the end of this chapter the reader will have a coherent description of imagination. Rather, it is quite likely that for some of my readers I may only provoke the sort of disorientation and sense of intangibility that this research regularly has produced in me. To be quite honest, most of the time I can barely make out the image of what I am trying to understand and reach for. There are brief flashes of understanding and insight when I know for sure that my search is hitting home with children: My data show me that, the children's achievements show me that, but then those fade into the background. In essence, most of the time my research questions are much too hard. Nonetheless, ever the optimist, my belief in the centrality of imagination to children's work pushes me to try to make this elusive process concrete, and at the same time to propose, as Binet (1911) puts it:

> a theory of action, according to which mental life is not at all a rational life, but a chaos of shadow crossed by flashes, something strange and above all discontinuous, which has appeared continuous and rational only because after the event it has been described in a language which brings order and clarity everywhere; but it is a factitious order, a verbal illusion. (cited in Donaldson, 1963, p. 28)

I hope my readers will give this chapter an imaginative reading, one that suspends for a time traditional conceptualizations of what research ought to be about and ought to look like. Join me, instead, as I describe a theory of action based on imagination. Consider with me how such a reading, filled with ellipses and discontinuities, might alter our views of literacy learning, research, and teaching.

IMAGINATION AND EDUCATION

The idea that imagination is a critical part of the educational process is obviously not new. At different points in the twentieth century, educational theory has embraced the arts, creativity, play, children's questions, and the idea that human intelligence is multidimensional and human expression multimodal. In the same way, much of my work as a teacher and a researcher had been circling around the workings of imagination. Over the years, I have built a teaching philosophy that places the arts and creative expression in the center of the curriculum, believing that play is a critical part of the learning process, and wonder the fuel that feeds our desire to understand the world. These beliefs have shaped my teaching and directed my research.

The use of imagination is not new to the field of education, but it remains, with a few exceptions, a peripheral subject. (For a notable exception, see Cobb, 1993.) We describe the ways in which teachers can support children's imaginative work and use imagination as a teaching tool, but we do very little to describe the workings of the process itself as it relates to our goals as educators. Most often the subject of imagination is approached through discussions of creativity, but, while imagination remains something that we vaguely know is important to many kinds of creative pursuits, it certainly is not considered a central part of basic literacy learning. While it is not possible in the context of this chapter to do an extensive analysis of the relationship between creativity and imagination, for the purpose of directing the reader's attention I would offer a simple distinction between creativity and imagination. Creativity most often is defined as a process of construction of the new, while imagination is a form of thought in which the new is brought to awareness. Both, therefore, have to do with generating the new, but creativity speaks to action in the world, and imagination speaks to action in the mind. I would propose, then, that in the context of this simple distinction imagination is both the precursor to the creative process and an integral part of it as it proceeds.

Although the subject of imagination has been a peripheral one in education, it has been widely explored by philosophers, artists, theologians, and scientists. Many artists have written explicitly about the development of their imaginative processes (for example, Coleridge, 1907; Grotowski, 1968; Lewis, 1956; Paz, 1990; Sartre, 1964; Stevens, 1960). Philosophers and theologians have considered the role of imagination in learning, in perception, and more broadly as a way to situate oneself in the world (for example, Bachelard, 1971; de Chardin, 1960; Greene, 1995; Sartre, 1961; Warnock, 1976). Scientists have spoken or written about the role of imagination in the development of their work (for example, Cobb, 1993; Fox-Keller, 1983; Holton, 1973; Medawar, 1982; Ochs, Jacoby, & Gonzales, 1996; Raymo, 1987; Root-Bernstein, 1989; Salk, 1983; Wolpert & Richards, 1997). Rarely, however, are their insights taken into account within the field of education and the life of the classroom. Only recently have a few scholars begun to direct their attention to the role of imagination in the process of becoming literate in a discipline (Warren, Ballenger, Ogonowski, Rosebery, & Hudicourt-Barnes, 2001), even though we have many firsthand accounts of the imaginative process at work in the lives of adults who have succeeded mightily in their respective fields. Those accounts are rich with descriptions of the role of imagination, and they speak to the issues of becoming an expert in a chosen field, of the processes at work in generating important theoretical and experimental breakthroughs, and of the connection between the inner world of perception, belief, and identity and the outer world of work and achievement.

Building an Inside-Out Theory of Literacy

As a teacher researcher seeking to find some form of guidance in making an elusive and seemingly illogical process logical, or at least tangible, to myself and others, I have found those firsthand accounts to be most useful. In developing a "theory of action" that speaks directly to the role of imagination in literacy learning, I also have been drawn continually to conceptual positions that offer what I would call "inside-out" theories of literacy.

In her seminal work on the teaching of reading, Sylvia Ashton-Warner (1963) clearly described her discovery that to be successful with Maori children, she had to exploit what she called the "volcanic vent" of the child, the child's inner source of creativity and violence (p. 29). Ashton-Warner's conviction gave rise to what she called the organic reading method and the use of the key vocabulary for teaching reading and writing. For Ashton-Warner, literacy was achieved by tapping into the center of her students' inner life and using their hopes, fears, fantasies, and conflicts to make words and the act of reading essential. As she writes in *Teacher* (1963):

> I see the mind of the five year old as a volcano with two vents: destructiveness and creativeness. . . . And it seems to me that since these words of the key vocabulary are no less than the captions of the dynamic life itself, they course out through the creative channel. . . . First words must mean something to a child. First words must have intense meaning for a child. They must be part of his being. . . . Pleasant words won't do. Respectable words won't do. They must be words organically tied, organically born from the dynamic life itself. (p. 30).

Ashton-Warner's identification of "the dynamic life" of the child moves me closer to defining the process I am seeking to understand. Note that she describes the creative process here as producing the words that are "the captions of the dynamic life"—but it is the center of the child's being that she is after, and her work goes on to describe a classroom where rich experiences were offered in all of the arts—with every experience intended to further what she called the alternating processes of "intake" and "output," or "breathe in" and "breathe out" (p. 89). In addition, over 40 years ago Ashton-Warner also identified the social as an integral part of literacy learning, complaining at one point, "From long sitting, watching, pondering (all so unprofessional) I have found the worst enemies to what we call teaching. . . . The first is the children's interest in each other. It plays the very devil with orthodox method. . . . In self-defense I've got to use the damn thing" (p. 103). Thus, the teaching of reading was tied both to the inner world of the child and to the outer world of the classroom where relationships powerfully influenced learning.

From a different tradition, James Gee (1990) has described literacy as a process that requires a student to essentially step into the shoes, for example, of a mathematician: to walk, talk, eat, and breathe mathematics. Thus, true literacy is achieved when an individual lives in the body of a subject, identifying with it in a visceral way and translating that identification into action in the world. It requires both mastery of the subject itself, and a public presentation of self as expert. One must believe and know, and one also must convince others.

Madeline Grumet (1988), in proposing a theory of "bodyreading," unites the positions of Ashton-Warner as teacher and Gee as sociolinguist. Grumet looks deeply into the meaning of reading as a broad cultural practice embedded in the particularities of each individual's social, physical, and emotional life—a practice that she believes has been cut out of the process of schooling. In her conceptualization of the disjunct between the individual and the school, she locates the center of learning organically, as do Ashton-Warner and Gee.

> In "bodyreading" I borrow this body-subject to run some errands, to bring what we know to where we live, to bring reading home again. To bring what we know to where we live has not always been the project of curriculum, for schooling . . . has functioned to repudiate the body, the place where it lives, and the people who care for it. (p. 129)

Here Grumet clarifies the importance of identity, drawing attention to the interaction between the "dynamic," inner life of the individual and the public world of school. She uses the image of reading as living in "the body" to convey the sense that reading is not a process that takes place above the neck, but is rather an all-encompassing, visceral activity.

These theories challenge me as a teacher and a researcher to find a way to peel back the layers of the literacy onion, as it were, from the outside in, and identify the natural, ontological processes of discourse acquisition at work. First I must consider what is organic and natural to the learner. Then I must figure out how to corral that for the purposes of deeper learning. In the process of responding to that challenge, I have identified the child's imaginative life as central to the process.

Why Imagination?

My desire to understand imagination began with a teaching problem. In 1994 I met Denzel, a second-grade, African-American child. Suffice it to say by way of summary that Denzel, a child who was healthy, happy, intelligent, and serious about school, but who had not been read to in his home, learned to read in second grade, but could not be engaged in listening or responding to literature at read-aloud time. I spent one teaching year looking carefully at the meaning and function of storybook reading and exploring Denzel's, and my other students', perspectives on that very central part of early literacy teaching (Gallas, 1997). By June, I had concluded that Denzel did not have the ability to imaginatively project himself into the life of a read story; and I also had observed repeatedly that he could not deeply engage with many other kinds of classroom texts to advance his own learning.

At that point I began to view imagination as a critical component of literacy learning, and as a teacher I went on to focus more clearly on the kind of learning that I considered to be the goal of my work with children. Denzel helped me to see that what I wanted for my students was to take them beyond basic skills that "toe at the edges of literacy" (Gallas, 1997, p. 253), to move them toward a deeper understanding of the texts, talk, and semiotic tools that lie at the heart of each discipline (Lemke, 1990; Smagorinsky & Coppock, 1994). I felt I had failed Denzel because I had not been able to build an explicit bridge to that kind of involvement. However, it was precisely that sense of loss and inadequacy that pushed me into a deeper consideration of the topic of imagination.

Imagination as a Question

Below is an excerpt from my field notes written consecutively during the last week of school. It shows how, after 9 months of inquiry into storybook reading, I identified imagination as a focus for future inquiry.

> I've been very distracted by Denzel and what I perceive to be some kind of failure on our part (his and mine) to crack this thing called school. I want to feel like he has entered the meta-discourse on thinking and learning that the other children move so freely through—the one that combines intellect and creativity, that uses imagination to enter new subjects, or books, or poems. I don't feel that I've gotten him to that point where he is developing a knowledge of higher-order thinking and how one accesses that. What is it that I want from him? It seems to be a particular kind of mindfulness. How to define it?
>
> *Tuesday:* We have our summer—baby—birthday party. Parents bring in great food: sushi, cake and strawberries, cookies, cupcakes, juice, and jello. Ayako's mom made a raspberry jello that was just beautiful: layers of white and red gelatin.

Denzel had four servings. We went outside to play, and half the class started to make up a line game that sort of resembled Red Rover, but was a line that, like an ocean wave, chased, and then enclosed whomever it caught. They were chanting nonsense rhymes, laughing and falling. Denzel and Alex came out a little late and they watched for a few seconds. Then Denzel came over and asked me if he could go and play catch with his cousin, who was also out on the playground with his class. I said "no," that I wanted him to play with our class. The children went under a big pine tree that was shady, and conferred. Denzel stood on the edge of the group, listening. Then the children broke apart running in goofy ways, making nonsense sounds. Denzel watched them for a minute, then followed running in a jerky, wobbling manner past me, and he had a big smile on his face, and called out, "Look, Karen, I'm running like jello!" He continued running after the group, then reached them and ran on. I stood still, trying to grasp the words, and shocked at the metaphor that had just come out of his mouth. Had I ever heard him use a metaphor before? I don't think so.

Wednesday: At recess I watched Denzel playing soccer with a group of boys using the entire playing field, which is huge, for their game. At one point Denzel was skipping backwards, anticipating the arrival of the ball. He was really skipping backwards as fast as he could with no one in sight. Then he tripped, fell, rolled over once backwards, jumped up with a huge smile on his face, and continued skipping backwards.

Thursday, the last day of school: We usually have a private class recital. That means that anyone who wants to perform, can. Children dance, sing, play instruments, do impersonations. When I asked in the morning who wanted to perform, about half the class responded, including Denzel. My intern, Cindy, and I surveyed what the children would be doing. Denzel said he would be doing a dance. That afternoon we gathered in the auditorium, sitting in two levels of chairs around the piano. When Denzel's turn came, he got up, went to the center of the empty space, and announced, "I will do a dance from karate. And it's called 'The Lion.' But I won't do the song." He then performed a very beautiful series of movements beginning with a crouch, transitioning to back rolls and somersaults that propelled him around the edges of the audience in an arc. Then he sprang up onto all fours and crawled slowly across the center of the space growling in a low, even . . . Was it a purr? A lion's purr? Our mouths dropped at this, and the children, who had been absolutely silent, bent forward imperceptibly to see him, wondering, I think, as I was, whether they were hearing things! Finally Denzel stopped, dropped lower to the floor, and then raised himself up on his knees with his hands resting on his lap. "Done," he said. We applauded, still somewhere between wonder and bewilderment. Then Denzel announced, "The Snake." He began a less choreographed version of the movement of the snake, including more rolls, half somersaults, a dance clearly emerging from the martial arts. But this one seemed different from the first. I could have sworn he was improvising. (Field Notes: June 16–23, 1994)

What I saw Denzel do in those last few days of school negated my judgments about his lack of imagination. Clearly imagination was there working for him on a very sophisticated, aesthetic, and intellectual level, but it was working outside of the "units" of words. For Denzel, movement was a way to imaginatively understand his world, but one that I had missed in spite of careful watching and talking for 9 months. I realized that I had made yet another chauvinistic assumption about the ways in which my experience of the world was naturally congruent with that of all of my students. I had done that many times before, always in the process of carrying out classroom research on early literacy, but this time the assumption had been around something that seemed even less tangible than linguistic or cultural differences. After this final observation, my questions emerged clearly. What does imagination look like in its different forms? How does it work for children who are different from myself? Where does it fit in the process of literacy learning and teaching? How does one pursue a study of something as permeable as imagination?

> Everything man does that's worth doing is some kind of construction, and the imagination is the constructive power of the mind set free to work on pure construction for its own sake. The units don't have to be words; they can be numbers or tones or colors or bricks or pieces of marble. It is hardly possible to understand what the imagination is doing with words without seeing how it operates with some of these other units. (Frye, 1964, p. 119)

As Frye points out, in order to fully understand what imagination was doing with words, I needed to broaden my notion of the forms it took in everyday life.

RESEARCH METHOD

To consider imagination as a topic to be investigated, I realized that I had to start with my own life since I had never paid close attention to the ways in which imagination functioned for me. From July 1994 through the summer of 1995, a year in which I was not teaching, I kept a journal about my own experiences of imagination, using personal experience as a way to expand my view of the subject. I contemplated, for example, the problem of understanding pure movement as an imaginative form, recording what passed through my mind when I took my daily 2-hour walks, when I danced, when I swam. In early December, as I walked along a desolate stretch of Gloucester, Massachusetts, coastline, the following words popped into my head. They ran on for a while, repeating themselves and gradually expanding as new phrases were admitted until they finally came fully to consciousness. I stopped by the side of the road and wrote them down as fast as I could.

> Once this coast was common land, covered only by spanses of wooly briars, old man's beard, bursting clouds of filament, wily oaks, and crackling bittersweet. They ran from the edge of the beaches, just behind the tufts of sea grass, straight across hills of granite and pine—forever. The only way in was from the rocky coast, and it offered no knowledge of how to pass through. There were no paths, only deer run and the low, damp tunnels of the ancient box turtles. In this land, I live, with little memory or imagination. My sight of that time is limited to night frights and small moments of delight in the objects cast off by the ocean.

That is only partly true. There is a quality of imagination that admits me to other worlds, that begins stories about things or people I see, and that lets me build their story around some random (or purposeful?) act, one I only happen upon. But those stories are only beginnings. They never end because, as I said, my imagination is a small one confined mostly to night frights, and flights of bizarre fancy. I begin these stories and then, because their endings would be either too filled with joy and resolution (something I have never understood) or too perverse (something I fear), I abandon them. And besides, they unfold only in my head. The texts are never more than vines of story, starting and stopping, then unwinding in quieter hours. This kind of text represents a part of what I was trying to bring to awareness. By studying my own experience of imagination, I felt I could begin to pull the phenomenon apart and develop new categories within it. In fact, over the year I did begin to identify a number of different ways in which my imagination was functioning, recording examples over time of fantasies, delusions, wonder and questioning, play, dreams, songlines, movement patterns, fears, and more. I began also to discover the ways in which those functions had positive or negative effects on my daily life and on my own learning. For example, an excerpt I noted in my journal illustrates a case in which my imagination interfered with my learning. In this instance, I had been learning to scuba dive and was having my first class using scuba equipment in water. Although I had wanted to learn for a long time, every now and then a bit of panic would seize me as the thought of not breathing air naturally passed through my mind. What I was aware of was the lack of control in the endeavor. In other words, if everything went well, this new pastime was a snap; but if something went wrong . . . , well, my imagination ran amuck with the possibilities. I was definitely in trouble, my imagination overrunning my logic. The whole thing had hints of mortality about it. I was fine until I went down, breathing as I'd been taught, but the quality of the breaths was alarming. There wasn't enough air, just as I'd imagined. I became claustrophobic and signaled that I had to surface. By the beginning of the next school year, through the process of bringing different parts of my own imaginative life to consciousness, my understanding of imagination was considerably broadened, and the vastness of its influence in every area of my life was apparent. I believed that the next step would be to begin watching children.

Data Collection in the Classroom

In the years since 1995 I have continued to inquire into the workings of imagination, focusing on the children in my primary classroom. I have collected data very widely using transcripts of audiotapes and interviews, and field notes from both structured classroom experiences such as sharing time and science, math, and reading lessons, and more unstructured expressive times when my students choose their own activities, with very little orchestration on my part, in areas such as dramatic play, music, art, and block building. In both structured and unstructured class time, I acted as a participant-observer, actively taking field notes on an Alpha Smart Pro and/or audiotaping our classroom interactions. During classroom events in which I was directly involved either as a teacher or as a co-actor, my field notes were taken later in the day when I was not teaching, from as little as 30 minutes to as long as 6 hours later. Often, if there were details of physical description or dialogue that I believed were significant and a tape recorder was not going as the event was unfolding, I would jot down snatches of conversation on Post-it notes to use as prompts for my later writing. Generally, my students knew that I regularly recorded in writing or on tape what they said and did.

The problem of researching something as intangible as imagination prompted me to begin watching in a different way what children were doing. Instead of identifying a specific question in thinking about literacy, I began simply to look for evidence of imaginative work wherever and whenever it occurred. One might characterize this as watching for what Anne Haas Dyson (1993) would term the "unofficial" work of children, except that I made new spaces for imagination to emerge in my classroom, thus bringing it into the official realm. I wanted to get a broad picture of imagination from the child's perspective and so I changed my practice to accommodate my research question. To accomplish this, I have had to create a classroom environment where my students have an unusual amount of room to flex their imaginative muscles, as it were, so that I have opportunities to observe and document their work. There are times when I join them in their exercises, participating in their dramatic play, painting with them at the easels, joining in their fantasy games, and at all times eavesdropping on their conversations and collecting what they leave behind. This is my research methodology at this point in time. I follow their trails, act as a participant-observer, and try to be aware of the range of what they are doing.

Participants and Setting

The children whose work will be cited in this study come from two different research settings. Denzel and two of the focal children, Emily and Sophia, were my students at a large, public elementary school in Brookline, Massachusetts, an urban community on the edge of Boston. That school is culturally and racially diverse and has more than 550 students in grades K–8. The remaining children cited in this study are students in a small, rural charter school on the central California coast. This school serves a relatively homogeneous Caucasian population and has approximately 150 students in grades K–8.

The physical design of my classroom in both settings reflects my long-standing belief that elementary classrooms should be richly provisioned and provide many different kinds of spaces for learning and teaching. Thus, my classrooms include active play spaces that adjoin one another and encourage children to eavesdrop and extend their dramatic play and classwork into different areas and media, as well as quiet-work tables where children can work alone or in small groups. The materials in the classroom are displayed on open shelves where children can easily handle them, and include resource books, natural materials, the "tools" of the classroom and of study (for example, magnifying glasses, rulers, staples, scissors, hole punchers, tape, etc.), assorted papers and writing instruments, manipulatives, and a variety of art materials such as colored pencils, chalk, markers, paints, clays, stencils, and stamps.

Although my students do not have assigned desks, they each have several cubbies where different kinds of ongoing work are stored. The classroom also includes a large meeting area, usually bordered by a small couch or comfortable chair. In this space whole-class meetings, sharing and group discussions, and small- and large-group instruction take place. Group stories and poems are composed; students present their work; stories are read; and various kinds of manipulative games are played. Thus, the physical space of the classroom reflects my desire that my students and I be aware of everything that is going on in the classroom.

IMAGINATION AND IDENTITY

In the process of linking my questions about imagination with an inside-out theory of literacy, I seek to describe what entering a discourse through the imagination means and how that entry becomes public so that I, as a teacher, can see it happen and take it from one level to another. When imagination is being used in the service of developing an identity, for example, the identity of a scientist, how does it look? The problem with this kind of inquiry is that schools are not naturally places where we allow spaces for imagination to enter into the process of discourse acquisition, so that even I (who have been looking for it carefully and systematically) sometimes either just plain miss it, or squelch it for the purposes of maintaining order in the classroom. It is like searching for a moving target.

One of my guiding questions for the past 3 years has been this: How do children begin to walk in the shoes, for example, of a scientist? What does that look like? Typically, I come across a part of the answer in the following manner. During visits to the SciTechatorium, the hands-on science museum located on the campus of the charter school where I taught kindergarten, I observed two of my kindergarten boys spend three separate sessions, over a 3-week period, developing an elaborate fantasy around a large telescope that was part of an astronomy exhibit. The exhibit itself included the telescope; models of the space shuttle; a tile from one of the shuttles; posters of planets, the different shuttles, the sun, and so on; and a timeline of space exploration, among other items. On one particular day, the two boys were starting to extend their fantasy to all parts of the museum, and were running around as if chasing aliens. I approached them to curb this behavior, based on my split-second conclusion that pretending is hazardous in a place full of precious exhibits. In the midst of my intervention with them I stopped, realizing the absurdity of what I was saying given my commitment to the place of wonder and imagination in the scientific process. I apologized for having interrupted and urged them to continue with their play, but to try to limit their movement around the museum. They happily agreed and continued on while I ran to get a pencil and paper, and began to take down their talk. After that incident I looked around and realized that every single child in my class was doing the same thing all over the museum. Some were more public about their fantasies, some were completely silent, but all were building imaginary worlds using the exhibits in the museum as the catalysts, and most, in an incipient way, were assuming the role of the scientist in their explorations of those worlds.

Here is a typical transcript from two children working in a fossil exhibit. They were using small brushes to uncover molds of fossil remains that were covered with sand. Around them were books on dinosaurs and fossils, posters, and many different kinds of fossils.

> *Clara:* (displaying a page of a book to the others and speaking authoritatively) These are the animals we're looking for. I want you all to take a look.
>
> *Maura:* (speaking with a British accent, and pointing to the fossil she is uncovering) Look, Clara, over here, it's completely flat.
>
> *Clara:* I'm not sure what that is.
>
> *Maura:* This is way too special for people to have. (She picks up a book and points to a picture.)
>
> *Clara:* That is not the same as the picture.
>
> *Maura:* Oh gosh! I think it's a T-Rex! We're going to be famous!

These kinds of observations helped me to more clearly define the kind of work I had seen Emily doing 2 years earlier in her conversations with, and pursuit of, insects. When I recorded the field notes that open this chapter, I did so because I knew Emily was working with her imagination. However, my conceptualization of the work she was doing was limited to simply taking note of her actions. I did not at the time draw the relationship between her imaginative work and the scientific process. Clara and Maura, however, and the dramatic play of my other students helped me to make the connection between imagination and the development of the scientist's persona. Here, for example, Clara and Maura were working with identity on two levels. First, they were becoming archaeologists by orchestrating a performance about the work of archaeologists and taking on what they perceived to be the appropriate tone and posture for that work. Then, as part of that process they were relating to their material, that is, the props in the museum, in a scientific way. Note Clara as she compares the bones being uncovered with the drawing of the dinosaur in the book: "That [meaning what Maura was uncovering] is not the same as the picture." Clara used her analytic skills to propose that the skeletal remains of the mold could in no way be the same as the animal illustrated in the book. As 5-year-olds, these girls were beginning to play out a process that Medawar (1982) points to in his description of the actions of scientists.

> Scientific reasoning is therefore at all levels an interaction between two episodes of thought—a dialogue between two voices, the one imaginative and the other critical; a dialogue . . . between the possible and the actual, between proposal and disposal, between what might be true and what is in fact the case. (p. 46)

In the same way, Emily became the scientist in her play with insects and also used many of the tools that scientists might employ as she worked with the insects, with me, and with her peers. She observed her insects and bugs meticulously, sketched them and recorded details about their development (as we have seen earlier in this chapter), constructed elaborate environments for them, and spoke authoritatively about their habits. And while an observer might have mistaken her understanding of the role of fantasy when she was talking to her ants and inferred that she was completely immersed in "pretending" (as I most certainly would have prior to this study), Emily was quite clear about what she was doing. When asked if the insects really "talked to her," she admitted that it wasn't really "talk like people do," but that they were "telling" her things. Note the following exchange I had with Emily one morning before school. The principal and I were sitting on a desk chatting as the children began to come into the room. Emily came up to us and told us that her praying mantis had died.

Teacher: Did she make an egg case before she died?
Emily: No, but I asked her if she had laid eggs. And she told me
she laid them before I caught her.

What I had to conclude, after observing her for a school year, was that
the "telling" came from Emily's close and continuous observation of
insects. For example, the brief sharing-time excerpt that follows reveals
how systematic and analytic her observations were.

Sharing-Time Field Notes

Emily shares some crickets that she keeps as pets, and as food
for her now-dead praying mantis. Her knowledge about them is
extensive. She speaks of the difficulty of telling them apart and
points out that an injury "like if they have a lost wing or something, makes it more easy" to tell them apart. She hypothesizes
that females are lighter color and have no wings.

Emily's work was very congruent with the descriptions we now have
from scientists of their childhood experiences of the world. For those
who are deeply involved in the study of the natural world, that study
often begins at an early age and the relationship that develops is one
of a close and organic identification with the creatures and the phe-
nomena of that world (Cobb, 1993; Fox-Keller, 1983; Holton, 1973).
More compelling, however, are descriptions of scientists working as
adults in the laboratory using imagination to enter the physical world
they are studying (Ochs, et al., 1996; Salk, 1983; Wolpert & Richards,
1997). In these accounts, the "I" of self moves into the body of the
phenomenon under study. As Sir James Black, a Nobel Laureate, states:
"You then try and pretend that you are the receptor. You imagine what
it would be like if this molecule were coming out of space towards you.
What would it look like, what would it do?" (Wolpert & Richards, 1997,
p. 126).

IMAGINATION AND DISCOURSE APPROPRIATION

As I have expanded my observations of children's imaginative
work, I see that imagination is a process through which children take
control of their experience so that the events, texts, and tools they
encounter in school become part of their bodies and are re-expressed
through the force of their actions. If given the opportunity to place

the world of school into an imaginative context, young children begin to appropriate the words, symbols, and tools of the different subject areas for their own purposes, very much in the sense Bakhtin (1981) has proposed when he writes of how a speaker must "populate the word . . . with his own intention, his own accent . . . adapting it to his own semantic and expressive intention" (p. 294). That process of appropriation, however, depends on the teacher's ability to provide a wide variety of props specific to the subject under study, as well as an exposure to "cultural tools" (Smagorinsky & Coppock, 1994) that further the student's inquiries. Those tools assist students in building the bridge between their experiences of the "now" of classroom texts with which they come in contact through the process of instruction, and the future of new texts that they themselves create.

I would propose that the process of discourse appropriation occurs when students are enabled to use an array of cultural tools to "access" their imaginative worlds and take control of the texts and the ideas they encounter. That kind of process requires that different kinds of expressive and temporal spaces be created within classrooms. For example, in October 1998 I observed an interesting phenomenon in my kindergarten classroom. One morning, a small group of girls noticed a large box of maps that had been placed prominently on a bookshelf since September, and they decided to go on a "trip." They set up a row of chairs as if they were airplane seats, unfolded the maps, and spent about 30 minutes "going to California." About 2 weeks later the maps came out again, but this time about 14 children joined in the travel fantasy in groups of five and six, segregated by sex. As with the first time, they lined up chairs and spent a great deal of time scrutinizing the maps. This time, however, they also began to make their own maps, drawing on their laps while they traveled, as if recording their itinerary.

I talked to all of them quite extensively about what they were doing, and they were able to describe what part of the journey they were on as well the status of the other trips going on in the other groups. But essentially my moves as a teacher, beyond the initial strategic placement of the maps as props in the room, consisted of talking with the children about their intentions as they worked, and then prompting them to share their new maps at the end of each day. The map work continued for about 5 days, and the children produced piles of maps on their own, sharing at the end of each morning. Throughout the year, they returned to the maps intermittently, always using them with three components: imaginary trips, the handling and "reading" of real maps, and the invention of new maps of their own. In March, during their last round of map work, two girls invented new kinds of maps of which they made copies for me when they saw my evident interest in trying to understand what they were doing. Here is how they described their new maps and their purposes in designing them.

> First we found the maps and then we wanted to make our own maps. So we copied from the maps how to draw. Then we started to go on a trip, and then we made calculators on our maps! The calculators reminded us of the telephone and then we put on a TV. If we don't have a telephone, we couldn't call, and we needed to count stuff on the calculator. If we say something on it [keypad], like . . . , "Is someone having a birthday party here?" . . . it will say "no," or "yes," and where it [the party] is. We also made a key for the whole world to unlock wherever you go, and to lock it back up whenever you go away.

The girls also added a real writing pad for notes. All of these, including the keypad, calculator, telephone, and TV screen, were drawn or built onto the maps, resulting in a three-dimensional effect. Through this process, which continued over a 6-month period, these 5-year-olds imagined themselves into the world of geography using the props I had supplied for them and the tools of drama and art to build a new conception of what a map might be in the world they would grow into. In looking closely at the ways in which their maps evolved, I could see that they were imaginatively taking control of the map as both a text and a tool, and reconfiguring both the design and the future of maps in their lives. This work was about imagination, and it was also about power and control.

AUTHORING

There is also a part of the process of discourse acquisition that is fundamentally social. The work I have observed in my classrooms would not continue to recur without the rich social interactions that surround it. When the children's work with texts, props, and cultural tools becomes public and is created with full knowledge that it will have a public viewing, it moves into the realm of "authoring." Over the past few months I have come to define authoring as the process of metaphorically "writing" the world in a way that gives that interpretation of the world weight, voice, and agency, a way that has the ability to influence the thinking, feelings, and actions of others.

One thing that distinguishes authoring from the pure exercise of imagination in an introverted, egocentric sense, is that it is an event in which an individual creates a new text and intentionally attempts to influence an audience. The text can be oral or written, a painting, a dance, or a song; it can be an explanation of the solution to an equation, or a theory about the world. What distinguishes the text is that the author presents it to an audience in a public way, essentially for some kind of validation. To me, authoring represents a movement toward the core of discourse acquisition. It is the point at which imaginative identity merges with discourse appropriation: One must believe and know, and one must convince others. In other words, literacy encompasses a private and a public identity. It requires that a person be able to create public texts that influence others, and it is most clearly social work in which the student learns about presentation of self and the importance of "reading" an audience and influencing the thinking and feelings of that audience. As Bauman (1977) points out in his description of performance,

> Performance involves on the part of the performer an assumption of accountability to an audience. . . . From the point of view of the audience, the act of expression on the part of the performer is thus marked as subject to evaluation for the way it is done, for the relative skill and effectiveness of the performer's display of competence. (p. 11)

Yet authoring also arises directly from the imaginative process itself and in this way represents the physical incarnation of imagination as it comes in contact with the world. Every painting, sculpture, performance, poem, and story that is presented to an audience begins with an imaginative response to the world, but the desire to communicate that response involves its own kind of "suspension of disbelief." Essentially, the author must imaginatively take on a public persona (Gallas, 1998) and risk failure and public humiliation for the purposes of expression and communication. As any performer, public speaker, or educator knows, that kind of risk taking requires a giant leap of faith and a powerful sense of the role being played.

When I first began researching imagination in my classroom, I was fortunate to have a class of wildly creative first graders. Within that class a 6-year-old Italian-American girl named Sophia became a focal child for me as I tried to document how children used the imaginative process in different areas of the curriculum. Sophia was a most remarkable child whose work in every expressive domain was tremendously compelling to others; she had a great ability to capture an audience's attention through performance and hold it. For example, the following sharing-time story offers a look into the ways Sophia used an improvised story as a vehicle for performance and social control.

Sharing Time: March 14, 1996

(Sophia begins by rubbing her hands together, as she smiles mischievously and slowly surveys the audience.)

Sophia: Once upon a time, there was a little girl named Sophia, and she called all of her friends. She called (names every girl in the audience).

Ayasha: No boys!

Sophia: And then I called all of the little boys to come and play with me. (The boys cheer.) I called (names all of the boys in the class). All the little boys were there, and Johnny went swimming. We were going to meet him there. Then we had a little party and we ran into the middle of the street. And the cars were going "Vroom, Vroom, Vroom!" and then I went out and put a little stop sign so the children could cross the street. We went to the beach and I jumped into the water, and it was so hot! And I got Brenden a sea star. . . . There was a little man there, who started walking down the beach. And all of the sudden the little man fell! He was so teeny, that teeny little man, that he fell into the sand and drownded! In the sand! And then I stepped on him. Then I picked him up by the foot, and threw him in the water. He said, "Help!" Then Ruth picked him up. She found a clam that was closed. She opened it up, and there wasn't anything inside, so she put the little man in, and threw him out to sea. Then the little man's wife and family came. And there were 13 of them! So we found 13 clams, and guess what we did then?

All: What?

Sophia: We put all of 'em in a shell, and threw them out to sea with the little man!

Like all of her stories, this story was socially inclusive, but Sophia remained clearly in charge of the story and her performance. (Note, for example, her response to Ayasha's bid for control.) Here, Sophia took an everyday experience that all the children enjoyed and added an element of danger that she, as the narrator, heroically anticipated, and resolved. The story also includes violence, something Sophia, who was a diminutive, feminine girl, specialized in, a fact that constantly delighted and horrified the boys in her audience.

At the time I began to watch Sophia, I also was completing a study of the dynamics of power and gender in the classroom, and had been working with the notion of performance and persona as a way to understand the dynamic social life of children in school (Gallas, 1998). As I watched Sophia at work, she was soon joined by two other powerful and imaginative girls who also began to use improvised storytelling to gain powerful positions in the class. These girls solidified my belief that performance was an integral part of children's social interactions, but they also caused me to think more deeply about the concept of audience. In my work on gender and power, I had seen clearly that most children in my first- and second-grade classes were acutely aware of the reactions of their audiences to their social maneuvering. Some even knew how to control or manipulate their audience. Yet as first graders, Sophia and her two classmates had an understanding of audience that was more fluid. They intimidated, cajoled, charmed, and repudiated their audiences, depending on their aesthetic and social purposes. Their understanding of the relationship between audience and performer stood out for me, but at that time those understandings seemed to be unrelated to my inquiry into the imaginative process.

In 1998, I moved to California and found myself teaching kindergarten in a small, rural charter school on the central California coast. My interest in exploring the manifestations of imagination continued in this new setting, and I was able to expand my data collection to include 5-year-olds. Of my 20 students, all but four had attended preschool for at least 2 years. The four children who had not attended preschool, Sabrina, George, Joe, and Margie, represented families with very limited incomes. Otherwise my students were middle class and upper middle class. I identify these children because, as the reader will see, their work in kindergarten, especially when considered in the context of this chapter and of my evolving questions about imagination and literacy, provided a significant contrast to that of their peers.

At the beginning of the school year, I set out to tape sharing time, as I had since 1989. I sat and waited for the children's stories to emerge in my kindergarten and offered many different kinds of opportunities for storytelling and dramatic performances. Nothing happened. My students were active in drama and blocks—they were making up stories in the contexts of their play in those areas—but when faced with an audience of their peers, they did not naturally tell a story about anything. In fact, they had very little to say at all. There were, however, a few notable exceptions: Sabrina, Margie, George, and Joe.

The second week of school, Sabrina, Margie, and George began to use the last period of our morning—the part labeled "stories and songs"—for performances. These began one day in response to my query as to whether anyone had a song to sing for the class. I said it could be a song they had already learned, or one they just made up. In response, Sabrina immediately stood up and asked if she could sing "a song about love." She began to sing and directed me to play my guitar as she sang. As I changed chords, she very naturally changed her songlines to accompany me, completely improvising lyrics and melody. The other children were quite surprised and clapped when she was done. I then asked for another song, and Margie got up and sang a song about the sky and the clouds. When she was done, the children clapped and I asked Margie if she had made up the song or been taught it, and she said she had made it up. At that point George, who had said pointedly he did not like songs and had climbed up in the loft while the girls were singing, came down and signaled that he, too, had a song. He came over to me and directed me to play, and as I started he began to do a very beautiful martial arts dance. The children were completely taken aback and thought he was being funny, and some began to laugh. George stopped dancing and began to cry. When I explained to George that the children were just surprised by his dance, he dried his tears and said he'd try again. He had not drawn a distinction between the words "song" and "dance," and had interpreted as congruent the girls' songs and his own desire to move to my guitar chords. He then performed another dance, which the other children were able to watch and appreciate.

This event began to recur regularly with the same three children as regular performers. The rest of the class continued to watch, but were unable to create these kinds of spontaneous texts for others. However, the efforts of Sabrina, Margie, and George now represent to me a first move into the authoring cycle. Sharing time, though, continued as it had been. Most of the children took a very passive stance, presenting an object to the class with a few short sentences, for example, "This is my rock. I got it at the beach," and then waiting for the class to respond. The children continued to be active in drama, blocks, painting, and unstructured dramatic play, but virtually all of their work in these areas was private work. Each time I attempted to pull the private dramas into the public space, they could not make the transition.

The following text marked the beginning of a kind of interactive storytelling style that occurred in different forms, always through the agency of these four children.

Sharing Time: November 11, 1998

George: (sharing a toy bat) This is my bat, and this its tail. I got this at Burger King. Questions or comments.
Dan: Which Burger King? The one that has a lot of hamburgers?
George: The one with chicken.
Sabrina: What movie is he [the bat] from?
George: Anastasia.
Dan: Once there was a bat and he lived in the rainforest.
Margie: And a dinosaur came and almost ate him and he flew so fast he couldn't ate him.
Sabrina: One time there was Anastasia in the movie and the guy had a hat like that.
Joe: There was some long teeth sticking out of the tree, and it was a T-Rex. (George had been trying to speak but the speakers were coming in too fast for him to intervene.)
Teacher: George, would you like to try one?
George: Yes. There was a dog named Ruby [the name of my bassett hound], and a dog named Ruby found a bat. This bat. This one I have in my hand. (Smiles broadly, and the children laugh out loud.)

During this same time period, Joe, who is a gifted artist, began to use the sharing chair as a vehicle to feature his art and tell long stories, which held the children enthralled. Following is an example of the kind of text he would create:

Sharing Time: November 19, 1998

(Joe is sharing a book he has illustrated at home. It is quite long, including about 20 pages of drawings.)
Joe: This is a Utahraptor book. The kind like in Jurassic Park. This raptor isn't real. He's a robot. (Children begin to comment and talk about the first picture.)
Mark: Can everybody hold their comments!
Joe: (pointing to page 1) Does he look happy? He ate a dinosaur. (page 2) He's dunking down, so nobody can see him. When people come by, he's jumping out. (page 3) You think that's how big a T-Rex is to a person? (page 4) Lookit what I got in there. Lookit what the man threw in there! Threw a bomb. Do you think it's going to blow up a robot? (page 5) Lookit! The toy robot. That's the thing his toy robot does. Loookit

what's coming up ahead! A raptor shadow. (The class' comments are getting quite rowdy, with action noises going on and lots of talk about the art.) I'm not going on until everyone is quiet. (The group immediately quiets.) (page 6) Do you think that thing is gonna kill . . . ? (Suddenly looks up at his audience, wide-eyed, making a funny face.) Whoops! I forgot to draw his head! (lots of laughter from the audience) (page 7) See, see him up in the tree? (page 8) Do you think he looks hungry? (page 9) Lookit what the raptor threw on his arm. The raptor is up in the ceiling. There was this big rock on the ceiling and it fell on him. Some of his robot is crushed.

Joe's performances began to resemble the work that I had seen Sophia and her friends doing 2 years earlier in my first-grade class. Although Joe lacked Sophia's fluency and skill as a storyteller, his intentions in influencing and controlling the audience through his art were well defined. In this case he used the turning of the pages to control the pace of his narrative and the amount of time he had as the presenter. Later, he stopped the momentum he had created to restore order so that the audience once again could focus on his drawings. As an artist, he had learned through previous sharing experiences that his illustrations anchored his audience's attention and gave him status in the class.

Still, in spite of the storytelling performances of these few children, the rest of the class did not begin to make a similar shift toward creating public stories. However, a few things began to develop in the first week in December. Three girls, Clara, Molly, and Leila, found the materials in the writing center that had been there for months and began to use them, writing letters to one another and to their moms, stuffing shipping labels (which they called "checks") in the envelopes, and sealing them. The same day, Leila and Bobbie were in the housekeeping corner with Sabrina, and I overheard them talking about their "hotel" and restaurant. They were lying on the floor staring at themselves in the mirror, dressed in bouffant skirts, hats, and high heels. I casually walked over and asked them if they needed a business manager to help them make a menu for their restaurant. They were unanimously in favor of that, and I sat down with them and took their dictation, writing up a menu with prices. They then took an order from me and I was served tea and muffins.

The next day at our reading meeting, I showed the menu and asked the girls to describe their restaurant. I also asked the letter writers to describe their activities. At choice time that day, things began to develop. Robert and Troy, who had never before shown an interest in the drama corner, went right to it, set the table for the restaurant, got me to tie carpenter aprons around their waists, went to the writing center and picked up some checks, wrote their names on the checks, and pasted them to the front of their shirts. Several other children went to the writing center and began to compose "letters," mostly pictures for their mothers, using copious amounts of envelopes and stickers for stamps. Again I visited the restaurant and asked for a table. The boys were quite surprised and asked me why I was there. I said I was there to eat and was waiting for a friend to join me. Robert escorted me to a table, gave me the menu, and waited for my order. I noted that he didn't have a pad to take my order on, and went and got him a thick, short pad of paper. As I ordered from the menu, he carefully copied the words and prices from the menu, then tore the paper off the pad and passed it to Troy, who cooked the meal. By that time they were joined by Dan, who served me my meal. Before I ate, I asked for a telephone, saying I needed to make a call. Once again they were quite surprised, but they handed me the phone. Here is my text:

> Hello. Yes, this is Karen. Well, where are you? I've been waiting a long time, and I'm hungry. I don't care if you're stuck in traffic, we had a date and you're very late. Well, I'm just going to go ahead and order. Bye.

The boys had listened to the whole conversation. Dan served my "shrimp" and then went over to the phone, picked it up, dialed a number, and proceeded to have the following conversation:

> Are you bringing that stuff we need? When will it get here? Tell me when you're here and I'll come and unload the truck.

A short time after, Sabrina asked for the phone, dialed, and began a conversation as her meal was served. At the time, I was only slightly conscious of the relationship between my decision to join in the drama with the children and my desire for them to bring their private dramas into the public domain. Later, in looking at the outcome of these series of events and in further defining what authoring meant to me, I realized that the teacher and the teacher researcher were acting in concert. I had joined in their dramas for the purpose of bringing them into the public, or official, world of the classroom. What I saw was that my performance enabled many children to expand their own performances, and further that my request that the products or texts of their dramatic work be shared, had a snowball effect. In essence, these 5-year-olds began to widen their lens and take notice of what was around them; they began to see what Margie, George, Joe, and Sabrina already knew, that there were personal and public benefits to working with an audience. (Or perhaps I might propose that the other children began to remember what they had once known but had forgotten, or unlearned, in preschool.)

The following week, sharing time began to change. What changed, however, was not that the children began to tell stories, as I had expected, but rather that performances were co-constructed using the object or picture that the sharing child presented. This change initially was orchestrated by Margie. In most cases, what was developing was a sort of comedic series of exchanges in which the sharing child played the fool while also explaining her picture or adding detail to her description of the object. The following example was orchestrated by Margie with the help of her audience:

Sharing Time: December 10, 1998

Margie: (sharing her art journal) This is me. This is my dog with a tree. These are the flowers and the little birdies. Questions or comments.

Sabrina: Where's the sun? (Margie looks and points to the corner of the picture.)

Mark: (claps)

George: Well, I used to have a dog but it's old.

Thomas: Um, why is your head so tall? (Margie turns the book around, stares carefully at the picture, looks up and laughs as she shrugs.)

Leila: Um. Um. Where's your body? I see just your hair, but (Margie points to the body, which is hard to see from the audience.)

Justin: It looks like you're gone cause the sun, it's so bright!

Joe: You're disappearing!

Margie: (turns the book around, stares at it for several seconds, looks up as if surprised) Ahhh! (The class laughs out loud.)

Sabrina: It looks like you're all yellow!

Margie: (turns the book around, stares, looks up with the same look of surprise) Ahhh! (The class laughs, this time louder.)

Brian: I can't see your eyes and your mouth.

Margie: That's because they're too light.

Sabrina: Are you throwing a ball for your dog?

Margie: Yeah.

Sabrina: I don't see the ball!

Margie: (looks at the book, then up at her audience) Ahhh! (The crowd laughs again.)

Joe: Where's your nose?

Margie: (same routine) Ahhh!

Dan: That's a good tree. But why didn't you draw the branches?

Margie: (turns the book, stares harder, looks up, eyes wider) Ahhh! (The class breaks up. Boys are rolling on top of each other. Girls are hugging each other with excitement.)

In the days that followed, Margie's "Ahhh!" routine was adopted and adapted by a few other children for their own purposes. The children introduced extensive word play and verbal jousting around the definitions of what their objects or pictures did or didn't mean. Sessions like this soon expanded to include all of the children in the class as both initiators and interactive audience members. By May, many children who had been silent and self-conscious during more improvisational performances were improvising songs and orchestrating dance and musical events. That signaled to me that the children had made a movement toward understanding their roles as co-performers, as well as the potential social benefits of the authoring process. Both audience members and the sharing child created texts as they went along, becoming mutually aware of both the pace of the exchanges and the uses of hyperbole, understatement, humor, and audience response.

Often these sessions ended with a breakdown of order and general hilarity, which I could not control. My response to that loss of control was not teacherly in that I didn't try to wrest it back. Because I wanted these children to be more active in the development of the public discourse of the classroom during sharing time and our "stories and songs" meetings, I knew that using my authority to control the social outcome of the authoring process would derail their efforts. And to be quite honest, a part of me liked the loss of control: It was funny and spontaneous, and the end result was a kind of joyfulness that deepened the links in our community and expanded the children's expressive repertoire.

Of course, readers of Bakhtin (1984) will recognize the elements of "carnival" in this description, and although my students were creating a carnival atmosphere in the style of kindergarten, the issues that surround carnival as a public event were obviously present in their work. In creating space for the idea of authoring, I also created what some researchers have characterized as a potentially dangerous textual space where children's meanings and intentions as authors are left unexamined (Lensmire, 1994, 1997; Swaim, 1998). Certainly, as control of the public discourse continually shifted from child to child through the authoring process, the established authority in the classroom, in this case that of the teacher, was purposefully undermined, making the dynamic both exciting and risky. And while this particular class of children did not use these occasions to manipulate or attack others, I have observed classes that did (Gallas, 1998). What I learned from those occasions, and what I have observed in this research, is that dynamic dialogic communities cannot be created unless I, as teacher, embrace the authoring process and all its risks. That process of creating a public text serves as a gateway to the development of my students' public identities as individuals who influence the thinking, feeling, and imaginative worlds of their peers. As control over the public discourse moves from child to child to teacher to child, and back again, every member of the community participates in constructing, critiquing, and reflecting on the texts being created. In this kind of framework for learning and instruction, scripted pedagogical practices must give way when they encounter the action of children's imaginative responses.

"LOOK, KAREN, I'M RUNNING LIKE JELLO!"

For literacy to become an inside-out process that is driven by imagination, it must be "organically born from the dynamic life" of students (Ashton-Warner, 1963, p. 30) and allow them to bring what they know to where they live (Grumet, 1988). When Denzel ran past me and announced that he was "running like jello," he was showing me where he lived, and that event occurred because I was ready to see it. In the same way, Emily, Sophia, Sabrina, George, Margie, and Joe brought their dynamic inner lives into the classroom and made them public because a discourse space had been created for them to carry out their own purposes as learners. At every point in this research, children have offered public demonstrations of imagination at work in the service of their learning. Their actions compel me, on a daily basis, to shape the conditions of public discourse and my textual expectations with them as co-authors.

This is a caveat that I believe all literacy teachers, who in my mind include teachers of all subjects at all grade levels, pre-K to graduate, must take up. Writing as I am from the state of California, where curriculum is conceived and then legislated by policy makers in cooperation (collusion?) with textbook publishers, a state where schools may buy instructional materials only from approved lists, and where literacy learning is expected to be programmed according to the tick of the clock, the notion of viewing literacy curricula as beginning with the imaginative life of the student moves from one that stands on the fringes of educational practice to a point of heresy. However, if language and literacy teachers do not rise up and begin to stand on the heretical edges of their profession, students like Denzel, rather than being pulled, body and soul, into the life of the classroom, will remain forever marginalized, living a vivid and dynamic imaginative life but never finding the bridge that connects that life to the world of school.

Imagining the Classroom

Cathy O'Connor

I.

Writing an afterword can be a delicate task. An afterword can easily be construed as "the last word" on the book, a summative evaluation of sorts. In a volume containing reports of teacher research, an afterword written by a university-based researcher might be read as an attempt to provide validation of the contents.

In the months during which this volume took shape, a question came up about what contribution I might make. Starting in 1990, I attended the majority of the BTRS meetings. I was there when Steve Griffin spoke, with great puzzlement, of the child who wrenched "sharing time" out of its doldrums with his odd and compelling epics, tales that emptied the sharing time bleachers and ended with everyone on the field, so to speak. I was there when Roxanne Pappenheimer began to express apprehension about her decision to let her cooperating teacher bring "Night Kites" into her special education classroom. I was there when Susan Black, in mildly shocked tones, reported back to the group about her students' dislike of mainstreaming. I was there when the group first prepared to give conference presentations. And I read drafts of all the chapters, culminations of many "turns in the conversation." But I had never conducted teacher research. I have jointly conducted research with classroom teachers, and I teach my own students in a university, but these would not fit in as a chapter along with the others.

Someone suggested at one point that perhaps I should write a foreword or an afterword. Others didn't like this idea. As a university-based researcher, my afterword might be construed as an attempt to assess the value of this work, a valuation handed down from the academy. This I did not want.

But time passed, as it will when trying to bring a book to publication, and the group decided that, yes, perhaps I should try to write an afterword. And so I agreed, but I was left with the conundrum of how to offer an account of what I think is the very special—in fact unique—value of this work without seeming to offer an unasked-for summative evaluation. I will try to frame my remarks in a way that will show my great admiration for the work of this group, and my gratitude to them for what I have learned. In addition, I will try to characterize what this research offers that cannot be found in mainstream education research. Much of what I will say here has been said before by others—for example in the many publications of Marilyn Cochran-Smith and Susan Lytle. Yet I think it is worth reiterating these points for this volume in particular.

II.

Why should we read published research? Why not just rely on what we can find out for ourselves, or on what we already know to be true? This question would be nonsensical if posed about the physical sciences. New knowledge there is hard to get, and the tools and methods of science are heavy, expensive, and hard to wield. Consumers in those fields must wait for researchers to find out new things, theorize about them, and report them.

In education, however, this question seems reasonable to many. Why should we support or even read research on teaching and learning? Carl Kaestle (1993), in describing legislators' attitudes towards education research, says "Everybody's been to fourth grade, so everybody knows what good teaching is. You can't make your own ICBM or cure cancer, but you know how history should be taught and you know how kids should be disciplined" (p. 27).

More recently, voices from many arenas have called into question the value of education research of almost any kind. Against the gold standard of randomized controlled studies, virtually every published education research study is judged deficient. Federal agencies now call for such designs as a primary criterion for receiving tax dollars. Yet when education researchers actually pull off a large-scale, controlled, randomized study (e.g., Mosteller, Light, & Sachs, 1996), this, too, is attacked. For example, E. D. Hirsch (2002) rejects this study of class size for the very reason that others have held it up as a model: It ignores distinctions among individual classrooms. Hirsch criticizes the very source of its power and favors instead another kind of power—the close look at individual thinking provided in cognitive science research. He proposes a new model for education research: not the randomized controlled studies of medicine, but the laboratory studies of cognitive science. Hirsch sees this research as generalizable in spite of the particularities of individual learning.

Yet Hirsch's proposal can be subjected to the same criticism he levels at Mosteller, Light, and Sachs—results derived from the particularity of a case study, a "process tracing" of a problem-solver in a lab, does not yield universally applicable knowledge any more than a large-scale study of class size in a thousand classrooms does. Either may show us something important, replicable, and generalizable. But either can be shown to be "wrong" or "misleading" in any number of particular cases. And as many people have pointed out, if we look to education research for instrumental reasons, to find a solution for a problem, then we can never completely succeed, and never completely fail, because anything can be shown not to work for some students, and to work for others.

So is the generic classroom, that classroom where teaching and learning could be improved by generalizable findings, an unreachable fiction? Are classrooms irreducibly various—composed, as each one is, of a unique teacher and dozens of unique learners? If they *are* irreducibly various, then is there any reason to read, or even to conduct, education research? What can research tell us that cannot be learned in a few years of actual teaching, or in a walk through a school, or in asking the right questions of a few teachers? More to the point, how can studies like the ones in this volume—narrative, personal, particularistic—tell many different kinds of readers, teachers, researchers, administrators, what they need to know?

III.

The research in this volume might be called qualitative case studies. Many researchers who want to understand teaching and learning have used this form of study. Elliot Eisner (1991) poses the question: Can we learn lessons from qualitative case studies in ways that can be generalized to a variety of contexts? He and many others have argued that case studies achieve something like generality exactly *through* their particulars. Through such studies, we can envision a reality that exists most wholly in a fully drawn picture of the particular. We can enter into, and begin to imagine, a classroom by imagining one instantiation of it. Then, we can build new conceptualizations with which to understand many other, undescribed classrooms. Teaching and learning are exactly the kinds of domains that require further elaboration of this kind, because there are still so many things that we do not understand about how learning happens and does not happen in the complex environment of the classroom. The under-theorization that Hirsch and others complain of is a function of the complexity of these domains.

In the research of master teachers we gain access to intuitive and close-range knowledge about the nature of teaching and learning. This knowledge is about classrooms, not labs. In fact, some of the most compelling knowledge about teaching and learning could never be generated in labs. It concerns the multiple levels of interaction among students and teachers and classroom artifacts and lessons and curriculum and learning conditions. It is about how teaching and learning take place in mysterious, non-linear ways, in a moment or over a year. Relatively few researchers have taken on the challenge of systematically studying learning in classrooms. Those who have marvel at its complexity and try (usually in vain) to characterize what they observe.

Classroom teachers know this reality from the inside-out, from the first-person point of view. So when they reflect on their experiences, the results can be of value and of interest to many. However, systematic study of their own experiences, pushing beyond reflection to systematic observation, description, and sometimes explanation, is much rarer and more difficult but is of great value indeed.

It is through systematic studies like the ones in this book that we can begin to glimpse the complexity of teaching and learning in classrooms, and that we can begin to imagine what must be at play from moment to moment. And yet, like all humans, the vision of teachers is limited. Each study carries only a partial rendering of a tiny part of the universe of teaching and learning. In this, teacher researchers are not alone: No piece of education research, no matter who conducts it, and no matter how systematic, can present more than a tiny fraction of what we want to know. The reality to be described is too vast and too various. Yet, when a master teacher systematically studies what happens in his or her classroom, the work can provide the world with invaluable insights that are unavailable from any other source.

IV.

What kind of knowledge is it that a master teacher has? Cognitive science research tells us that master chess players do not operate on the basis of general algorithms. They work on the basis of tens of thousands of specific cases: Their brains are filled with examples, families of examples, classes of families of examples, induced from tens of thousands of hours of playing chess. It is knowledge of the particularities of many thousands of games that carries them through each new encounter.

What kind of knowledge is it that a master artist has? I am not a fan of Monet, but a few years ago a friend persuaded me to come along to an exhibit of his life's work. I walked through the halls, viewing haystacks and cathedrals and lily ponds rendered in all kinds of light, duly impressed but not particularly moved. Then, in the final room of the exhibit on one large wall were two huge paintings from the very end of Monet's long life. I had never seen them before, or, if I had, in reproduction they had not spoken to me. I was amazed to find that I was immediately moved to tears. However, the only words I can find to describe my impressions are the clichés that populate descriptions of the last works of great masters: power, serenity, effortlessness, depth, abstraction derived from a very deep seeing. These words convey nothing of the mastery displayed in the two paintings. Where did this mastery come from? It came from a great talent and many years of immersion in particular examples, studies and more studies, exploration and more exploration.

It is only through a deep understanding of particularities, forged through thousands of hours of exposure, that we can hope to gain deep mastery in a field like teaching. And yet even 10,000 hours of experience, 10 years of teaching, is not enough to yield a fully generalizable account of any major aspect of teaching and learning.

So what can those of us who are not in the classroom every day learn from the expertise and insights of these teacher researchers? I think the answer lies in thinking about what they want to accomplish as researchers. What do researchers want to accomplish, generally speaking? They want to find something out to their own satisfaction, and by writing about it change other people's thinking or expand other people's knowledge. So what is it that these teachers want to understand and convey to others through their authoring?

Without attempting to reduce their motives, or to claim that I know what drives them, I will tell what I have seen in their attempts, again and again. In each of these chapters, the writer is attempting to understand, by an imaginative reconstruction based on children's words and actions, what is going on as these students engage with, or refuse to engage with, the instructional context. That context has many edges— the edge of interaction between student and other students, between teacher and student, between student and text; the interactional vertices and interstices of any classroom are innumerable. And it is in these spaces that the teacher's work succeeds or fails. A master teacher is constantly considering evidence of a very fragmentary sort as he or she attempts to understand what is happening in the minds and interactions of the students.

In each chapter (and, in fact, in almost all of the work of the seminar members that I can recall from our 10 years of meetings) there is a concerted attempt by the teacher researcher to project him or herself imaginatively into the experience of the student; to figure out, as far as is possible, what it is that the child might be experiencing and how they might be thinking about the situation.

Is this simply a case of an admirable empathy for one's students? I think it is much more than that. I think it is the locus of a special knowledge that this type of teacher research can offer to the field. It exists in the teacher's privileged position with respect to the conditions of student learning. And these studies are efforts by these outstanding teachers to understand more clearly what happens as a child takes up what is happening around him or her and transforms it.

As Ann Phillips points out, many of the "turns" in the group's work began with a puzzling moment. This is often, I have observed, a moment in which a student says something completely unintelligible, or does something strange or maddening, or seems to be operating in another dimension. Such moments, of course, happen in every classroom from preschool through graduate school. However, as the work of teaching cannot come to a halt to consider these moments, they usually pass unremarked and vanish into the torrent of other moments that make up each hectic school day. The teacher researchers in the BTRS, however, recognize that these moments are often the entry point to the possibility of deeper understanding. In my view, the deeper understanding the seminar members are attempting to build is about learning, the learning that takes place as a child brings him- or herself into contact with other people's words and actions.

In education research, the ultimate questions concern the nature of learning, what it is and how to make it happen. Refinement of teaching and reform of schooling more generally have as their goal only the improvement of learning. So in "mainstream" educational research we have studies of teaching, studies of curriculum, studies of instructional methods and arrangements of schooling, and studies of student performance. But with very few exceptions researchers cannot make much headway at the actual nexus of learning—the interface where the instructional context is encountered by the students, with all of their history and knowledge and predilections and reasons to approach or avoid what the teacher is offering. Whatever one's beliefs about learning, it is clear that learning happens (or fails to happen) for each student, moment by moment, within the complex milieu of words, objects, ideas, and face-to-face interactions in the classroom. It is also clear that often we cannot see the results of learning or not-learning. Even the most exhaustive performance measures may fail to reveal what some children have learned or not learned. So teachers are often left with the nagging questions: What have they learned? What is happening in their minds? What is happening here in this classroom among these students?

V.

It is against this background that I think we can see the value of the efforts of each of these teacher researchers to understand what lies beyond the fragments of linguistic and interactional data with which they work. The expertise they have comes from thousands and thousands of hours spent with students, each interaction adding to their ability to sense, to predict, to adapt to the unique qualities, strengths, and weaknesses of individual students. When such experts focus intensively on the moments of learning and not-learning, and the moments of uninterpretable response, their analyses are informed by the insights and knowledge derived from those thousands of hours. Moreover, the subjects of their studies, their students, are deeply familiar to them, far more than they could be to any "participant observer," however attentive.

So in Cindy Ballenger's chapter, "Reading Storybooks with Young Children: The Case of *The Three Robbers*," we see her struggling to project herself imaginatively into the seemingly aberrant responses of her Haitian students. Why are they obsessed with the "piman"? Why are they obsessed with the moral status of the robbers? Why do they ignore the story in the book and persist in jointly making up their own episodes, even as she tries to read to them? We experience the impenetrability of their reasons and actions as Ballenger tries futilely to project herself into their ways of thinking. This frustration pushes her to make a move that provides illumination: She begins to consider her own ways with books and texts. Making her own familiar ways strange to herself, she projects herself imaginatively into her own experience! This move, and the subsequent reconsideration of the students' experiences of learning about texts and books, gives us the basis for renewed hope of envisioning something of what her students bring to the complicated space of her classroom. The imaginative questioning of one's self as *teacher* by one's *researcher* self is a strategy that took on a life of its own in the work of the group, and is found in other chapters as well.

Susan Black-Donellan, Cindy Beseler, and Roxanne Pappenheimer all puzzle about the experience their students are having in response to curricular and instructional choices that have been made for them. In Black-Donellan's case, she directly explores how her students feel about the day-to-day experience of being mainstreamed. In a testament to the strength of her desire to understand what her students are taking from their educational arrangements, her own presuppositions are replaced by what she learns. Through the sometimes opaque words of her students, she is able to see that her expectations about the benefits of mainstreaming do not match their experiences. Her ability to work with their words, to imagine what it must be like for them, gives the reader a glimpse into that fragile interface—where learning may or may not flourish for myriad reasons stemming from the students' experiences.

Cindy Beseler takes on an imaginative reconstruction of the construct of a "functional curriculum" in special education for young adults. As she follows her students in their sometimes funny, sometimes frustratingly incomprehensible, responses to a variety of schooling experiences, she discovers something that helps her: Her students use language in different ways within settings that they perceive as distinct. "Monday talk" and "Friday talk" are wonderful, rich exemplars of what sociolinguists might describe as different discourse genres. The purposes of the activity, the roles of the actors within that activity, and the resulting sense of self they gain in that setting, all lead to language variation of the kind that Beseler so insightfully interprets. The difference from the sociolinguist's account lies in Beseler's intimate knowledge of these students and her ability to project herself into what they are doing. Despite her protestations of puzzlement, in fact a reader outside can see a deep understanding born of her own intense observation and connection with these students. Her exploration of the effects of context on talk took on deep meaning for the group as a whole, as other members probed the ways in which context is a factor in shaping and in limiting performances of many kinds.

Roxanne Pappenheimer takes on the most difficult kind of learning—when the learner comes to understand that something about him- or herself as a person must change, that one must adjust to the world. For her students, this is tremendously slow and difficult. Her study of the way her young adult students take up the reading of a book is unlike anything I have ever encountered. What strikes me so powerfully about her account is that she is able to project herself imaginatively into the experience of students whose responses and behaviors are so problematic, so off-putting, so foreign to most readers. And yet that is clearly part of the reason that she was able to help them learn things that have changed the course of their lives.

Karen Gallas's work in the construction of a theory of action based in imagination leads to a chapter of great interest and complexity. Here I will only comment on the centrality of the "imaginative life of the student" in her classroom. As she makes room for it, and ponders the conditions under which she herself can see it and understand its role in the student's learning, we get a sense of the great intelligence, effort, and creativity that animate her own attempts to imagine the worlds of her students. Melding the work of Ashton-Warner, Grumet, and others with her own research on imagination, Gallas constructs an understanding of student literacy that resonates with those expressed in other chapters.

Jim Swaim leads the reader on a remarkable journey as he recognizes the stultification of a practice in his own classroom. His students, he realizes, are stuck in a mode of interacting that is actually constrained by his own pedagogical view of writing and of literature. As he creates opportunities for them to break out of this frozen practice, he projects himself into how his students see the new kind of writing as a world-creating act. As he comes to understand their new view, his own view dynamically responds. In this chapter we see a teacher researcher fearlessly exploring a very challenging problem, and displaying great powers of imagination himself as he ponders his students' own creations. Like Ballenger's work, Swaim's chapter centrally features an exploration of his own past understanding and of its transformation in response to the children's responses to him.

In Steve Griffin's chapter, he relates the story of his puzzled response to a student's strange form of "sharing." In large part because of his deep absorption in his students' experiences with him and with one another in his classroom, we were all able to participate in the discovery of this remarkable, spontaneous, discourse genre—which became known as "I need people" stories, or "inclusive stories." They started to turn up in other classrooms. In Swaim's chapter, we see them as Pamela includes all her classmates in the story of the mall stores. In Gallas's chapter, Sophia engages the audience through inclusion (as did Gia in Gallas, 1992). Children in Cindy Beseler's and Cindy Ballenger's classrooms also use public language in inclusive ways. All of these events are notably different from the normal ways of "doing school" and so seem puzzling or even problematic. But Griffin's early work on this started a line of research that the seminar members have continued. It is something that, I would assert, only teacher research of this kind could find and explore. It encompasses the curriculum, the teacher, and each of the children, along with the central child. It thus embodies the most complex aspects of the work of teaching, the coordination of these multiple intersecting dimensions and many consciousnesses.

The narrative quality of these works has been remarked upon by a number of readers in the past. Sometimes the narrative quality of certain types of teacher research is held up as a weakness, as though only the distanced voice of a traditional researcher can provide insights about learning. Instead, I would suggest that the narrative voice of the works in this volume stems from a deep and intimate knowledge, permitting the imaginative projection of these authors into the experience of their "characters," their students. These insights could not be gathered by anyone else. Perhaps there are other ways to report them, but the present narrative mode provides, in my view, a perfect vehicle for the kind of knowledge that only teachers such as these could provide.

This account would be incomplete if I did not mention what sets these narratives apart from many other seemingly similar narrative accounts. Each is based on systematic collection and analysis of data, in the form of tape-recordings, fieldnotes, and student work. Thus, each narrative is the product of working and reworking the writer's and the group's thoughts about the data. Different interpretations and conclusions were proposed, challenged, rejected, resurrected, rehabilitated, and rejected again. The process Ann Phillips describes created the space for this iterative reconsideration. The final chapters are, therefore, more than narratives stemming from observation alone; they are thoroughly considered works that can be challenged on the basis of the data that gave rise to them.

A final observation about these chapters: I have claimed that they differ from more standard education research by virtue of the teacher researcher's ability to imaginatively inhabit the experience of students as learners. But this does not give adequate attention to a central fact about this kind of research—the vulnerability of the teacher in researching his or her own classroom. In this way as well, this work goes beyond ordinary research. As Ann Phillips says, "If someone has opened herself up to scrutiny in the way found here, she is not merely arguing about ideas." I think that the striking quality of insight one finds in the work of the BTRS is underwritten, in part, by the openhearted commitment of these teachers to use their imaginations to explore that which is troubling, difficult, and potentially painful, and to share those explorations with the wider world of sometimes unsympathetic researchers. For that, among many other things, I offer them profound thanks.

References

Ashton-Warner, S. (1963). *Teacher*. New York: Simon & Schuster.

Bachelard, G. (1971). *On poetic imagination and reverie*. New York: Bobbs-Merrill.

Bakhtin, M. (1981). *The dialogic imagination* (C. Emerson, Ed.; C. Emerson & M. Holoquist, Trans.). Austin: University of Texas Press.

Bakhtin, M. (1984). *Problems of Dostoevsky's poetics* (C. Emerson, Ed. & Trans.). Minneapolis: University of Minnesota Press.

Ballenger, C. (1999). *Teaching other people's children*. New York: Teachers College Press.

Barnes, D. (1976). *From communication to curriculum*. Montclair, NJ: Boynton/Cook.

Bauman, R. (1977). *Verbal art as performance*. Prospect Heights, IL: Waveland Press.

Bloome, D. (1987). Research on reading as a social process. In D. Bloome (Ed.), *Literacy and schooling* (pp 124–127). Norwood, NJ: Ablex.

Bruner, J. (1986). *Actual minds, possible worlds*. Cambridge, MA: Harvard University Press.

Cazden, C. B. (1988). *Classroom discourse: The language of teaching and learning*. Portsmouth, NH: Heinemann.

Cobb, E. (1993). *The ecology of imagination in childhood*. Austin, TX: Spring.

Cochran-Smith, M. (1984). *The making of a reader*. Norwood, NJ: Ablex.

Coleridge, S. T. (1907). *Biographia literaria* (J. Shawcross, Ed.). London: Oxford University Press.

Corbin, H. (1969). *Creative imagination in the sufism of Ibn Arabi*. Princeton, NJ: Princeton University Press.

de Chardin, T. (1960). *The divine milieu*. New York: Harper & Brothers.

Delpit, L. (1986). Skills and other dilemmas of a progressive black educator. *Harvard Educational Review, 56*, 379–385.

Delpit, L. (1988). The silenced dialogue: Power and pedagogy in educating other people's children. *Harvard Educational Review, 58*, 280–298.

Donaldson, H. (1963). *A study of children's thinking*. New York: W.W. Norton.

Dyson, A. H. (1989). *Multiple worlds of child writers: Friends learning to write*. New York: Teachers College Press.

Dyson, A. H. (1993). *Social worlds of children learning to write in an urban primary school*. New York: Teachers College Press.

Dyson, A., & Genishi, C. (1994). *The need for story: Cultural diversity in classroom and community*. Urbana, IL: National Council of Teachers of English Press.

Egan, K. (1992). *Imagination in teaching and learning: The middle school years*. New York: Althouse Press.

Eisner, E. (1991). *The enlightened eye: Qualitative inquiry and the enhancement of educational practice.* New York: Macmillan.

Elbow, P. (1973). *Writing without teachers.* Oxford, UK: Oxford University Press.

Fox-Keller, E. (1983). *A feeling for the organism: The life and work of Barbara McClintock.* New York: Freeman.

Frye, N. (1964). *The educated imagination.* Bloomington: University of Indiana Press.

Gallas, K. (1991, February). *Making room for many voices: The Brookline Teacher Researcher Seminar.* Invited talk at the University of Pennsylvania Ethnography in Education Forum, Philadelphia.

Gallas, K. (1992, March). When the children take the chair: A study of sharing time in a primary classroom. *Language Arts, 69,* 172–182.

Gallas, K. (1994). *The languages of learning: How children talk, write, dance, draw, and sing their understanding of the world.* New York: Teachers College Press.

Gallas, K. (1995). *Talking their way into science: Hearing children's questions and theories, responding with curricula.* New York: Teachers College Press.

Gallas, K. (1997). Storytime as a magical act open only to the initiated: What some children don't know about power and may not find out. *Language Arts, 74,* 248–254.

Gallas, K. (1998). *"Sometimes I can be anything": Power, gender, and identity in a primary classroom.* New York: Teachers College Press.

Gee, J. P. (1989a). Literacies, discourse and linguistics. *Journal of Education, 171*(1), 5–18.

Gee, J. P. (1989b). The narrativization of experience in the oral style. *Journal of Education, 171*(1), 75–97.

Gee, J. P. (1989c). *What is literacy?* (Tech. Rep. No. 2). Newton, MA: Literacies Institute.

Gee, J. P. (1990). *Social linguistics and literacies: Ideology in discourses.* London: Falmer.

Gee, J. P., Michaels, S., & O'Connor, M. C. (1992) Discourse analysis. In M. D. LeCompte, W. L. Millroy, & J. Preissle (Eds.), *Handbook of qualitative research in education* (pp. 227–291). New York: Academic Press.

Greene, M. (1988). *The dialectic of freedom.* New York: Teachers College Press.

Greene, M. (1995). *Releasing the imagination: Essays on education, the arts, and social change.* San Francisco: Jossey-Bass.

Griffin, S. (1990a, August). *The teacher's perspective on the importance of thinking about language, culture and learning in the classroom.* Paper presented at the Literacies Institute First Annual Teaching as Research Seminar, Newton, MA.

Griffin, S. (1990b, September). *History of the Brookline Teacher Researcher Seminar.* Paper presented at the Modern Language Association Conference, "Responsibility for Literacy," Pittsburgh.

Griffin, S. (1993). "I need people": Storytelling in a second grade classroom. In *Children's voices, teachers' stories: Papers from the Brookline Teacher Researcher Seminar* (Literacies Institute Tech. Rep. No. 11). Newton, MA: Educational Development Center.

Grotowski, J. (1968). *Towards a poor theatre*. New York: Simon & Schuster.

Grumet, M. (1988). *Bitter milk*. Amherst: University of Massachusetts Press.

Guare, J. (1990). *Six degrees of separation*. New York: Vintage Books.

Heath, S. B. (1982). What no bedtime story means: Narrative skills at home and school. *Language in Society, 11*, 49–76.

Heath, S. B. (1983). *Ways with words: Language, life and work in communities and classrooms*. New York: Cambridge University Press.

Hirsch, E. D. (2002, October & November). Classroom research and cargo cults. *Policy Review*, pp. 51–69.

Holton, G. (1973). *Thematic origins of scientific thought*. Cambridge, MA: Harvard University Press.

Jarrell, R. (1964). *The bat-poet*. New York: Macmillan.

Kaestle, C. (1993, January-February). The awful reputation of education research. *Educational Researcher*, pp. 23, 26–31.

Kellogg, E. (1990, September). *On the collaboration of teachers and researchers: A teacher's perspective*. Paper presented at the Modern Language Association Conference, "Responsibility for Literacy," Pittsburgh.

Kerr, M. E. (1989). *Night kites*. New York: Harper Trophy.

LeGuin, U. (1989). *Dancing at the edge of the world: Thoughts on words, women, places*. New York Grove Press.

Lemke, J. (1990). *Talking science: Language, learning and values*. Norwood, NJ: Ablex.

Lensmire, T. J. (1994). Writing workshops as carnival: Reflections on an alternative learning environment. *Harvard Educational Review, 64*, 371–391.

Lensmire, T. J. (1997). The teacher as Dostoevskian novelist. *Research in the Teaching of English, 31*, 367–392.

Lewis, C. S. (1956). *Surprised by joy: The shaping of my early life*. New York: Harcourt Brace.

McCabe, A. (1997). Cultural background and storytelling: A review and implications for schooling. *The Elementary School Journal, 97*(5), 453–473.

McDonald, J. P. (1986). Raising the teacher's voice and the ironic role of theory. *Harvard Educational Review, 56*, 355–378.

McDonald, J. P. (1992). *Teaching: Making sense of an uncertain craft*. New York: Teachers College Press.

Medawar, P. (1982). *Pluto's republic*. Oxford: Oxford University Press.

Michaels, S. (1982). "Sharing time": Children's narrative styles and differential access to literacy. *Language in Society, 10*, 423–442.

Michaels, S. (1985). Hearing the connections in children's oral and written discourse. *Journal of Education, 167*, 36–56.

Michaels, S. (1987). Text and context: A new approach to the study of classroom writing. *Discourse Processes, 10*, 321–346.

Morson, G. S., & Emerson, C. (1990). *Mikhail Bakhtin: Creation of a prosaics*. Stanford, CA: Stanford University Press.

Mosteller, F., Light, R. J., & Sachs, J. A. (1996). Sustained inquiry in education: Lessons from skill grouping and class size. *Harvard Educational Review, 66*(4), 797–842.

Ochs, E., Jacoby, S., & Gonzales, P. (1996). "When I come down I'm in the domain state": Grammar and graphic representation in the interpretive activity of physicists. In E. Ochs, E. S. Schegloff, & S. A. Thompson (Eds.), *Interaction and grammar* (pp. 328–369). New York: Cambridge University Press.

Paley, V. (1986). On listening to what the children say. *Harvard Educational Review, 56*, 122–131.

Paz, O. (1990). *The other voice: Essays in modern poetry*. New York: Harcourt, Brace, Jovanovich.

Phillips, A. (1990). *What teachers need to know* (Literacies Institute Tech. Rep. No. 3). Newton, MA: Educational Development Center.

Phillips, A. (1991, February). *Hearing children's stories: A report on the Brookline Teacher Researcher Seminar*. Paper presented at the University of Pennsylvania Ethnography in Education Forum, Philadelphia.

Phillips, A. (1993). Raising the teacher's voice: The ironic role of silence. In *Children's voices, teachers' stories: Papers from the Brookline Teacher Researcher Seminar* (Literacies Institute Tech. Rep. No. 11). Newton, MA: Educational Development Center.

Phillips, A. (1994, April). *What is found there? The complexity of the teacher's voice*. Paper presented at the annual meeting of the American Educational Research Association, New Orleans.

Phillips, A., et al. (1993). *Children's voices, teachers' stories: Papers from the Brookline Teacher Researcher Seminar* (Literacies Institute Tech. Rep. No. 11). Newton, MA: Educational Development Center.

Raymo, C. (1987). *Honey from stone: A naturalist's search for God*. St. Paul, MN: Hungry Mind Press.

Root-Bernstein, R. S. (1989). *Discovering: Inventing and solving problems at the frontier of scienctific knowledge*. Cambridge, MA: Harvard University Press.

Salk, J. (1983). *The anatomy of reality*. New York: Columbia University Press.

Sartre, J. P. (1961). *The psychology of imagination*. New York: Citadel Press.

Sartre, J. P. (1964). *The words*. Greenwich, CT: Fawcett.

Scheffler, I. (1984). On the education of policymakers. *Harvard Educational Review, 54*, 152–165.

Smagorinsky, P., & Coppock, J. (1994). Cultural tools and the classroom context. *Written Communication, 11*, 283–310.

Smith, F. (1988). *Joining the literacy club*. Portsmouth, NH: Heinemann.

Stevens, W. (1960). *The necessary angel: Essays on reality and the imagination*. London: Faber & Faber.

Swaim, J. (1998). In search of an honest response. *Language Arts, 75*, 118–125.

Ungerer, T. (1991). *The three robbers*. New York: Aladdin.

Warnock, M. (1976). *Imagination*. Berkeley: University of California Press.

Warren, B., Ballenger, C., Ogonowski, M., Rosebery, A., & Hudicourt-Barnes, J. (2001). Re-thinking diversity in learning science: The logic of everyday languages. *Journal of Research of Science Teaching, 38*, 529–552.

Wells, G. (1986). *The meaning makers*. Portsmouth, NH: Heinemann.

Wells, G. (1991). Talk about text: Where literacy is learned and taught. In D. Booth & C. Thomley-Hall (Eds.), *The talk curriculum* (pp. 46–88). Portsmouth, NH: Heinemann.

Wilhelm, J. (1996). *"You gotta BE the book": Teaching engaged and reflective reading with adolescents*. New York: Teachers College Press.

Wolpert, L., & Richards, A. (1997). *Passionate minds: The inner world of scientists*. Oxford: Oxford University Press.

About the Contributors

Cynthia Ballenger has taught for many years, most recently as a literacy teacher in third and fourth grades with Haitian-American students. She is also a research associate with the Chèche Konen Center at TERC in Cambridge, Massachusetts. She has served on the board of the Spencer Foundation Practitioner and Mentoring Grant, and in other capacities to promote teacher research. Ballenger has published an account of her teaching of Haitian students in *Teaching Other People's Children: Literacy and Learning in a Bilingual Classroom,*which received the Outstanding Writing Award from the National Association of Colleges of Teacher Education.

   Cindy Beseler has taught students with developmental disabilities for a number of years. Her curriculum focuses on inclusion and transition from school to work. In addition, Beseler has co-facilitated a therapy group for young adults with disabilities and has presented at local and national conferences on topics ranging from preschool planning abilities and discourse patterns in science, to work with special needs populations.

   Susan Black-Donellan has been involved in special education for over 20 years. She has worked in school and residential settings. Mainstreaming is a special area of interest, and Black-Donellan has presented sessions on mainstreaming practices at a number of conferences. Presently she is coordinating services for students attending specialized schools in settings outside of public school systems.

   Karen Gallas is a teacher researcher who has taught children in the public schools of Massachusetts, California, and New Mexico since 1972. She received her doctorate in education from Boston University. Her work as a teacher researcher has focused on the role of the arts in teaching and learning, children's language in the classroom, the dynamics of gender and power in the classroom, and the process of teacher research. She has published papers in several journals, and three books, *The Languages of Learning*: *How Children Talk, Write, Dance, Draw, and Sing Their Understanding of the World; Talking Their Way into Science*: *Hearing Children's Questions and Theories, Responding With Curricula*; and *Sometimes I Can Be Anything: Power, Gender, and Identity in a Primary Classroom.*

Steve Griffin is currently a principal. Previously he spent 25 years as an early childhood and first- and second-grade teacher, and as a speech and language therapist. He was awarded the Caverley Award for Teaching in Brookline, Massachusetts. He remains deeply interested in the relationship between socioeconomic and cultural background and school achievement, particularly under standardized testing.

Roxanne Pappenheimer has taught students with a range of developmental disabilities for the past 23 years in preschool, elementary, and high school settings. She has been a guest lecturer and adjunct faculty at universities and colleges where she has shared her views on functional curriculum, the special education process, and school/family systems. She also has taught adult GED classes and courses on teacher research. Pappenheimer has served as a consultant at the Education Development Center in Newton, Massachusetts, in evaluating national standards for the assessment of special education teachers.

Ann Phillips taught fourth and fifth grades for 20 years. Her teaching and research interests focus on the epistemology of teaching and learning, arts as education, and teacher research. Her publications include *What Teachers Need to Know* and "Raising the Teacher's Voice: The Ironic Role of Silence," published by the Literacies Institute, and "Feeling Expressed: Portrait of a Young Poet," which appeared in *Language Arts*. She served on the editorial board of the *Harvard Educational Review* from 1989–1991 and co-edited an issue of the *Review* titled, "Arts as Education." She is presently at work on a dissertation for her Ph.D. at Harvard.

Jim Swaim has been an elementary teacher for over 30 years, the past 22 of them in the Brookline Public Schools. He is a founding member of the Learning and Teaching Collaborative, a school–university partnership and professional development model begun by teachers in 1986. He taught a course on literacy at Wheelock College and has presented his research in various national forums and has published in *Language Arts*.

Index

Actions of scientists, viii
Actual Minds, Possible Worlds
  (Bruner), viii
African-American students
  narrative structure used by, 3, 22–
    30
  poetic language of, 2–3
  referrals to speech/language
    therapist, 2–3
  sharing time as storytelling time,
    18–19, 22–30
  storybook reading of Haitian
    preschoolers, 1–2, 10–11, 31–
    42
American Educational Research
  Association (AERA), 20
Art, 144–145
Arthur (student)
  described, 46–47
  fixing talk and, 49–50
  Friday talk and, 51–52
Ashton-Warner, Sylvia, 15–16, 123,
  124, 146, 157
Authoring, 136–146
  art and, 141–142
  co-construction of performances,
    144–146
  dance in, 140
  defined, 136
  dramatic play and, 142–144
  music in, 140
  pure imagination versus, 137
  storytelling in, 137–139, 141–142
Author's chair, 78

Bachelard, G., 122
Bakhtin, M., 9, 135, 145–146

Ballenger, Cynthia (Cindy), 1–2, 8–
  11, 15–16, 20, 31–42, 122, 155,
  157
Barnes, Douglas, 7, 9, 15–16
Bat-Poet, The (Jarrell), 75–77
Bauman, R., 137
Beseler, Cindy, 7–8, 11, 43–70, 155–
  157
Best practices, 1
Big ideas, 8–9
Bill (student)
  described, 46–47
  Friday talk and, 51–53
  "Pepsi on the Rocks"
    conversation, 53–54
Binet, A., 121
Binocular vision, viii
Black, James, 134
Black-Donellan, Susan, 11, 106–118,
  149, 155–156
Bloome, D., 73
Bobbie (student), imagination and
  dramatic play, 142–143
Bodyreading (Grumet), 124
Boston University, 3
Brain damaged students. *See*
  Students with special needs
Brookline Teacher Researcher
  Seminar (BTRS), vii–xii, 14–20
  "bringing classrooms to the
    table," vii, ix, x–xi
  as collaboration between teachers
    and academics, 20–21
  concept of teacher research, vii
  early history, 2–4
  "freezing the action," 7
  initial funding, 3, 16, 20